SPIRITUAL G. P. S.*

A ROADMAP FOR YOUR SALVATION JOURNEY

by

Greg Hadley

*God Powered Solution

Hadley, Greg [1934 -   ]
A Spiritual G.P.S. – A Roadmap For Your Salvation Journey / Greg Hadley
1st edition

ISBN 10: 1-4922-2167-8
ISBN 13: 978-1492221678

Printed in the United States of America
First Edition

OTHER BOOKS BY GREG HADLEY

Fundamentals of Baseball Umpiring [1]

Common Problems; Common Sense Solutions

100 Everyday Epiphanies
    Simple Events That Can Inspire Prayer

God's Words to My Heart

Aging: The Autumn Phase of Life
    How to navigate through the Golden Years
    with grace and fulfillment

Twilight Reflections
    Where the Elderly Find God

Jesus Face-to-Face
    Tales of fleeting personal encounters with
    The Christ found in the New Testament Gospels

[1]In the National Baseball Hall of Fame, Cooperstown, New York

Please visit our website for further information.
www.gbhadley.com

DEDICATION

To my dear friend, Robert Ross ("Bob") Rogers,
held in esteemed memory.

TABLE OF CONTENTS

FOREWORD

In a sense I am the "Mother Founder" of the place that author Greg Hadley now calls home, Mary's Woods at Marylhurst, Lake Oswego, Oregon. It was my role, as the then Provincial Administrator, to call for requests for proposals, negotiate with the City of Lake Oswego for approvals, see that soil tests were done, and start setting the infrastructures in place. Returning later as a University Professor of Religion and Philosophy, I was inspired by resident Greg Hadley's wisdom and generosity as he participated in classes, liturgies, and held many responsibilities—while he also authored seven books.

A Spiritual G.P.S. reads like a combination meditation book and one of the wisdom writings of the Jewish Scriptures: especially *Sirach (Ecclesiasticus),* that wonderfully wise book on friendship, and *Proverbs*, those pearls of wisdom that help us realize and accept all of our human inclinations. The reader will be able to spend hours meditating on the quotes alone, which weave like beads throughout the text and make ready for the reflections that follow—quotes from scholars of many disciplines, as diverse as Lao Tzu, Nelson Mandela, J. K. Rowling, Thomas Aquinas, and A.A. Milne.

There are also sentences that are like prisms that reflect new ways of viewing realities. I found myself checking a few in the margins of the book. In considering the virtue of Hope, Hadley says, "Here is our dilemma: trust is the key to hope, but trust implies loss of control and most of us are uncomfortable letting go." Regarding the virtue of Generosity, I have heard expressions of "worthlessness" coming from women and men who are no longer working full time. The author's

i

words may spark them into the welcome act of giving in new ways: "Many of us have special skills that can be most helpful to schools or charities. Think about things like in-depth computer knowledge, financial planning or accounting expertise, medical or dental proficiency, organizational aptitude, vehicle repair competence and other skills." For those retired persons who complain that they are busier than they were when they worked full time, this insightful thought on the use of time may make us put a pencil to our calendars: "Some of us are like derelict old boats—we leak time like a boat leaks water. Just think of the time that evaporates each day on minor or meaningless tasks."

My favorite section is the chapter on keeping oneself educated. Perhaps this is because I am an educator and the over-55 "Mature Learners" in my classes tell me that they want to keep learning in order to "keep their brains alive." Too many persons seem to quit learning new skills and gleaning new ideas after they complete formal education, religious education programs, Confirmation, Bat/Bar Mitzvah preparation, or RCIA (Rite of Christian Initiation of Adults) sessions. As the great Karl Barth put it, "Prayer without study is empty. Study without prayer is blind." We pray to the God we know. This book, with an emphasis on the inherent connection between Reason and Faith, may just be one means for helping all of us "keep our brains alive."

I will want to use this book in the parish where I facilitate two groups, one a Grief and Bereavement group and the other a group of energetic Aging persons who have suggested topics very like those Hadley has anticipated in this book: forgiveness, sharing of time and talent, deepening one's spiritual life, augmenting one's theological and cultural education, writing an ethical or wisdom will, preparing for diminishment and death, and considering afterlife. The Grief group will want to consider further the value of and hope in this statement, "When we battle through the pain of grief and loss...we may find a gentle soul, beautiful in nature, which is calm, caring and very considerate of others." I suggest that readers may wish to use the book as a resource or guide for groups in churches, families, or community groups. I predict that it will facilitate a kind of sharing which is profound, significant, and moving.

Cecilia A. Ranger, SNJM, PhD
Educator, Spiritual Director, Retired Administrator.
Currently: Pastoral Assistant,
St. Mary Magdalen Parish, Portland, Oregon;
Author, History of Ecumenical Ministries of Oregon

Greg Hadley

PREFACE AND ACKNOWLEDGEMENTS

I was recently in New York at a family reunion with my six children and their families. One of the families lives in White Plains, a northern suburb of New York City. To all the rest the Interstate highways, major roads and surface streets in the area were totally unfamiliar. Several of the families had rental cars and there were many events planned that required travel to remote locations. I marveled as I watched my kids deftly figure out their travel routes using "smart" phones, iPads and GPS (Global Positioning Systems) devices built into the dashboards of the cars. These modern electronic wonders permitted everyone to get to all the places safely and smoothly...nobody got lost as far as I know. I have to admit that, as I approach my eightieth birthday, the latest level of sophistication in electronics has left me in the dust. I am resigned to accepting the fact that I must now rely on my kids...and grandkids...to get me to the physical places I need to be.

While watching the electronic wizardry around me, I started thinking about this book that I was in the middle of writing. The major theme of the book was about a road map or template folks could use to negotiate their own salvation journey. I hoped to write about the issues that people had to address in order to reach the end of their lives fully prepared for their next step into immortality. I was struck by the obvious analogy between GPS systems, Google Earth© maps and my writing assignment. Most of us need some directions to get from one physical point to another. For that we have maps, computers, Global Positioning Systems and the earth-circling satellites that make them function. Some of us may need some help navigating our spiritual journey through life. For that we can call upon a wide variety of sources—the Bible, the *magisterium*, or teaching authority, of the Church, an inspiring Pastor, effective spiritual direction, a consistent prayer life, devoted Christian companions and other God-centric activities. These things represent our own spiritual journey GPS—which I have re-named our *God Powered Solution.*

My book is not intended to compete with these other resources. I merely wish to offer a layperson's perspective about specific issues we should consider when planning the spiritual aspect of our lives. I hope this book will be helpful to you and serve as your own GPS. I wish to challenge you to think about and act upon the following fundamental things I believe directly affect our spiritual journey: Faith, hope, love, forgiveness, generosity, piety and prayer, religious education, your legacy, peace, acceptance and dealing with loss, care of your body and preparation for death and the afterlife. Some of these topics may resonate with you more than others. Feel free to use this book cafeteria-style, picking and choosing those sections that are most meaningful to you at the moment. Thank you for permitting me to share my ideas with you.

I have also found that wisdom quotes from the world's greatest philosophers, religious leaders, writers, politicians and influential people provide a perfect introduction to the major points I wish to raise. So many brilliant, thoughtful and visionary people have preceded us. Fortunately, they have recorded their wisdom for posterity. You will find quotes I have found from people such as Mother Teresa, Gautama Buddha, Robert Fulghum, Thomas á Kempis, Pope John Paul II, Aristotle, Martin Luther King, Jr., Gilbert Keith Chesterton, John Calvin, Elie Wiesel, Mohandas K. Gandhi, C. S. Lewis, Mitch Albom and many others. The wisdom quotes I have selected should not be considered merely as keys that open the door to ideas I wish to offer. I find them to be significant in themselves and recommend them to you for further contemplation and reflection.

Our view of reality is like a map with which to negotiate the terrain of life. If the map is false or inaccurate, we generally will become lost. If the map is true and accurate we will generally know where we are; and if we have decided where we want to go, we will know how to get there. The biggest problem with creating internal maps of reality is not that we have to start often from scratch, but if our map is to continue being useful, we must continuously update and revise it[1]. This is certainly true of our own salvation journey.

Our individual spiritual journeys are often difficult. The road we must travel is strewn with rocks, potholes and other daunting obstacles. Is there one among us who has not endured hurt, pain, loneliness, rejection, loss and suffering along the pathway? In spite of these things, the Christian believer marches along resolutely full of hope and awesome anticipation about the final destination. Our loving and merciful God has promised us that "Eye has not seen and ear has not heard what I have made ready for those who love Me." We do our best, relying on God's gracious assistance to finally reach the end of the human road living in His perpetual grace. As we take that final step from human life through the veil into immortal life, we hope to hear these words as we see God face-to-face: "Well done, good and faithful servant. Now enter into the home I have prepared for you in paradise." Perhaps our personal GPS has provided a path to that glorious moment.

Many thanks are offered to Sister Cecelia A. Ranger, SNJM, PhD, who wrote the Foreword. I feel extremely honored and grateful to Sister Cecelia who took time out of her very busy and productive schedule to participate in this project. I must acknowledge the wonderful aid given to me by Sister Peter Mary McInnis, SNJM who steadfastly supported me throughout the process of writing this book. Sister Peter Mary offered unfailing encouragement while patiently correcting my repeated mistakes in grammar and punctuation in my initial drafts. Thank you, dear Sister, for your love and faithfulness to me. The Chaplain at the retirement community where I live, Father Richard Berg, CSC is not only an inspired and beloved Holy Cross priest but I also count him as one of my dearest and most trusted friends. His gentle but direct critique of my work always lets me know when I have—and haven't—done a good job of writing. Thank you, Father Dick, for your consistently positive leadership, good humor and love as I travel my own personal salvation journey.

I must also lovingly acknowledge my wife and life partner, Evie, for her wonderful devotion to me. While I pound away on the keyboard of my computer doing my writing, she patiently keeps busy with other things awaiting the end of my day or evening creating words. Her faithfulness and love is beyond measure. I am deeply grateful for all she does.

Finally, thanks to each of my six children—Eileen, Mary, Leigh Anne, Bing, David and John—and their spouses and my fourteen grandchildren. They expect that each new book I turn out will probably be the last...only to find that another one is in the hopper. Perhaps this is the final book, but I am not sure.

Greg Hadley
Mary's Woods at Marylhurst
Lake Oswego, Oregon

CHAPTER 1

HOW ARE MY FUNDAMENTALS: FAITH, HOPE AND LOVE?

FAITH

Some come late to religious faith but many of us were raised in homes where belief was practiced, more or less importantly, as part of family tradition. From an early age, some of us were inculcated with a belief system that has survived much of our lives. Yes, as we left home and started life on our own the learned faith of our childhood may have waned, or even disappeared for a time, but waxed again as we reached an emotional or spiritual maturity. Our quest for metaphysical answers about who we really are, what relationship we have to a Creator and what life is all about led us back to some kind of faith experience.

This newly found understanding may not have been the same one we learned as children but that is of little importance. That we have discovered a set of beliefs that are comfortable to us is what counts. At least, it seems like that to me. I find it difficult to fathom how anyone can live his or her life successfully without any notion of mankind and its relationship to a Supreme Being, a Prime Source, a God. Here is where the concept of faith comes in. Once we accept the idea that there must be a God—even though we can't see Him or Her— we are required to embrace faith.

In Christian sacred scripture, we are told that the three most important virtues for us to practice are faith, hope and love. If these represent the fundamental aspects of human spiritual activity, it seems that we must complete a personal assessment of how well we are incorporating these virtues into our daily existence. We start with faith.

The Christian faith has not been tried and found wanting. It has been found difficult and left untried. G. K. Chesterton [2]

People have wide ranging experiences with personal faith so generalization is very tricky. Many were immersed as children in communal prayer, several trips to church each week, Bible studies, youth groups and other manifestations of the God-fearing beliefs of the family Patriarch or Matriarch. Others were raised in less devout homes where a belief in God was accepted, perhaps, but given less focus and importance in routine family life. Denominational affiliation influenced how much, or little, children were exposed to scripture, stories about God, family prayer and other religious practices. Then there were the luke warm families who dressed up to go to church on Christmas and Easter but that was about the extent of exposure to religion in those households. Finally there were the families where religious belief or expression was considered unimportant and was absent from family life. These examples only represent four points on a continuum of belief systems; all of us look at the notion of faith from a fairly unique perspective.

If you were raised in a faith-filled home, you may have experienced the rebellion against religion during your teenage years. "Church is boring...I don't get anything out of it...none of my friends go anymore." This sullen defiance seldom worked; you were dragged off to church on Sunday mornings or to religious education classes whether you wanted to go or not. Finally college arrived or a job that permitted you to live away from home. Now, on your own and marching to your own drummer, Sunday morning was a time to catch up on sleep and all the dreadful sermons and old hymns became a thing of the past for you. At least, this was true for many. Others continued the practices taught to them in their youth. But almost all young adults experienced some wavering or rebelliousness regarding faith. Now, as parents or grandparents themselves, these formerly insolent youths wonder why their children and grandchildren don't seem to embrace the faith they were taught. Why?

The quotation from Chesterton at the beginning of this segment provides one answer. Basic tenets of religions call for things such as turning one's cheek, loving your neighbor, taking care of the poor, abstaining from activities that may produce human pleasure and leading lives that are often difficult. The less motivated and those with weak faith may say, "Who needs all this religion? Life is tough enough without all these rules and regulations. God, please just leave me alone!" You know what? God may do just that. We have free will; God will let us exercise it freely.

Everyone would like to have a stronger faith. By themselves, the scriptures may not strengthen, but being faithful to what they teach does. In other words, faith cannot be separated from faithfulness.
John Bytheway

3

You may question whether or not everyone wants stronger faith. Even those who understand that deeper faith might entail spiritual risk still seek a better understanding of things that are not provable. Even though your faith may have waned in the past, don't you really want to believe in a God who created you, loves you and provides a sense of meaning to your existence? I believe, at a fundamental level, most people seek purpose in their lives. To the Christian, sacred scripture represents a major road map to all levels of believers. If you are one who is seeking a deeper faith, turn your attention to sacred scripture. The guidance for your life that you will find there can strengthen you spiritually. In turn, that may improve your faith. As the author says, "faith cannot be separated from faithfulness."

Faith is not desire. Faith is Will. Desires are things that need to be satisfied whereas Will is a force. Will changes the space around us. Paulo Coelho

Some seeking an increase in personal faith may drop to their knees and pray, "God, please send me the grace I need to improve my virtue of faith." All prayer is heard and is helpful one way or another. But it is not enough to just <u>want</u> an increase in faith; those seeking faith must personally <u>will</u> that to happen in their own lives. Perhaps a more complete prayer would be, "Lord, You already know that I seek an increase in faith. With all my heart, I am willing to accept whatever that increase in faith might mean in my life. Give me the grace to say 'yes' to whatever challenges increased faith will mean to me. I will that this happens to me, Lord."

Faith is walking face-first and full speed into the dark. Elizabeth Gilbert

Isn't Ms. Gilbert's statement descriptive and evocative? It speaks to the surrender of self to things that are unknowable. Consider the idea that there is an Almighty God and that He dwells inside of you. Fully accepting all the ramifications of this is pretty profound. If you truly admit this concept and consider all the things affected by your belief, life is forever changed. No longer are you in control; how can you be with a divine God in your life? Think of the ways you will change your human life now that you believe God lives in you. Can you possibly have the same relationship with family, friends and neighbors after fully accepting this article of faith? Yes, true faith forces us to walk at quick pace through a door into the total blackness of the unknown. We won't even be able to see if the room we enter has a floor. It is all or nothing. Faith conditioned by reservations is no faith at all. "I believe" permits no exceptions if it is real faith. How is your virtue of faith at this moment?

Doubt isn't the opposite of faith; it is an element of faith. Paul Tillich

Part of what it means to be human is uncertainty, the inability to always see things with crystal clarity and which fork in the road to select. Even those with seemingly unwavering faith in things eternal are occasionally overtaken with the issue of doubt. Particularly in times of distress, loneliness and pain faith can stagger or even collapse. "I am hurting; where is God when I need Him? Perhaps He does not really exist or maybe He does not love me as I thought He did." Is there one of us, in temporary agony, who has not thought those thoughts? But the richness of deep faith is highlighted by fleeting doubt. "I desperately need God right now, but I cannot find Him. Yet, I know He is here;

it is my human frailty that causes my faith to buckle." That drama has affected my life and, I suspect, yours too. I find myself limp and prostrate even after a lifetime of religious education, faithfulness to prayer and service to my church. How can my soul suddenly become so shredded by uncertainty? Doubt is a human condition; when afflicted by it, we pray more fervently, "Lord, help me with my unbelief." Don't fear your doubt; embrace it! As Miguel de Unamuno writes, "*Fe que no duda es fe muerta*," translated, "Faith which does not doubt is dead faith."

> *There were many dark moments when my faith...was sorely tested, but I would not and could not give myself up to despair. That way lays defeat and death.* Nelson Mandela

Few of us live lives that are nearly as momentous, stressful or meaningful as that lived by Nelson Mandela. He was thrust into a unique position of leadership during the time his country was undergoing a fateful and fundamental transition. Imprisoned for many years, Mr. Mandela must have undergone numerous crises of faith. Despite this testing, he emerged as a forceful, charismatic leader who led his country successfully during a crucial period. We who have our faith tested in less dramatic ways can look to Mandela as a positive example. We, too, may face dark moments when our faith is sorely tested. In those times, remember Mr. Mandela. He would not and could not give in to despair. Neither can any of us.

> *Faith and reason are like two wings of the human spirit by which it soars to the truth.*
> Great Pope John Paul II

Many of us make a basic mistake when considering the virtue of faith. The error consists of separating faith and reason into disconnected concepts that have nothing to do with one another. This is incorrect. Voltaire said that faith consists in believing when it is beyond the power of reason to believe. While that may be true, much about our faith is reasonable. It is true that the existence of a Supreme Being, or God, is not provable. Yet St. Thomas Aquinas in his *Summa Theologica* made a convincing and powerful case through his Seven Proofs that the existence of God is eminently reasonable. The quote from John Paul II advises us that faith and reason work together inside our human spirit to help us find the truth. The gift of faith we possess is not blind. The fact that we cannot prove something doesn't make it wrong.

Faith is about doing. You are how you act not just how you believe. Mitch Albom

We hear in St. Matthew 7: 21 (New American Bible), "Not everyone who says to me, 'Lord, Lord,' will enter the kingdom of heaven, but only the one who does the will of my Father in heaven." We can ardently profess our faith in words, but it means little unless we live in accordance with our belief. If our faith teaches us to love our neighbor, care for the poor, welcome strangers, respect life and all those other things embedded in our personal creed, then we must live those beliefs by performing them daily. Truly, we are not just what we say we believe, but also what we do each day.

**To one who has faith, no explanation is necessary.
To one without faith, no explanation is possible.**
St. Thomas Aquinas

and

With faith there are no questions; without faith there are no answers. Yisroel Meir Ha-cohen

These two quotes, one from a famous philosopher and saint and the other from a distinguished Jewish Rabbi, sum up our understanding about the virtue of faith. There is one important point to be made: our faith is a gift from God, freely given to those who have done nothing to deserve it. To keep this gift flourishing in our souls, it is up to each of us to nourish our faith and keep it vibrant and growing. Nothing says that God cannot withdraw this gift. How many of us know of someone who had the gift of faith but lost it through lack of care? To those of us blessed with faith, ask God for the grace to keep this virtue alive in your heart. If you have lost, misplaced or never had the gift of faith, humbly ask God that you be blessed with this faith.

God does not require that we be successful, only that we be faithful. Mother Teresa

This final quote is for those who are sometimes discouraged about faith.

CHAPTER 2

HOW ARE MY FUNDAMENTALS: FAITH, HOPE AND LOVE?

HOPE

What exactly is hope? It seems to be a simple enough word that we often use in daily conversation. When one is asked to define hope, this may not be so easy. The *Webster's Encyclopedic Unabridged Dictionary* advises that hope is "the feeling that what is wanted can be had or that events will turn out for the best." So far so good, at least from a secular perspective. The Catechism of the Catholic Church provides a more spiritual definition. Hope, the Catechism tells us, is the theological virtue by which we desire the kingdom of heaven and eternal life as our happiness, placing our trust in Christ's promises and relying not on our own strength, but on the help and the grace of the Holy Spirit. The Catechism goes on to say that the virtue of hope responds to the aspiration to happiness, which God has placed in the heart of every person...it keeps us from discouragement, it sustains us during times of abandonment; it opens up our hearts in expectation of eternal beatitude.

How does hope apply to your daily circumstances of living? If a family member tells you about a relative's serious illness, a feeling that with good medical care and lots of prayer everything will be okay may soon follow your initial distress. On more mundane matters, we know that winter's rain and gloom will soon be followed by fresh spring weather and beautiful flowers. We feel certain this hope will be fulfilled. We all eventually reach that time when we began to clearly see the final horizon of our earthly life. Is there one of us who does not fervently hope that a merciful God will make a gentle final judgment of our life and lead us to His side in paradise for all eternity?

Hope does not begin when our intellect is formed or end when we breathe our last breath. We are told that God now dwells within each of us. We also believe that happiness in eternal life consists in being in the presence of God forever. Since God is present to us now, doesn't that mean our hope to be in God's presence forever has already begun here on earth? Doesn't that also mean that the hope we now have will extend to all eternity? How do you think about hope especially in the face of human discouragement you sometimes experience with your spiritual life? Are you full of hope even when things look hopeless? This is what we are called to be; our courage comes from God's in-dwelling.

Hope is a verb with its shirtsleeves rolled up.
David Orr

Sometimes our cries for help can be quite plaintive: Please don't let that medical test be a sign of health trouble ahead; my budget cannot afford another repair bill so let my car keep running; let my grandchild pass that important school test; help my child with the difficult marriage situation he is facing. All these fervent prayers about current human problems are based on the virtue of hope. We ask for assistance while simultaneously believing—and hoping—that everything will work out for the best.

Similar scenarios apply to our spiritual life, too. Help me overcome this habitual failing that afflicts me; show me how God loves me unconditionally even when I cannot love myself; let me understand how my current spiritual aridity will eventually come to an end. To overcome many of these human and spiritual problems, we must roll up our sleeves and get to work as Mr. Orr suggests. Often it takes our hard work and resilience to make hope a viable option in our lives. Frantic hand wringing and tearful pleading must be replaced by hard-nosed conversation with God. "I am dealing with a serious problem here, Lord. I know you are at my side but I need some help from you so I can hope you will take care of everything I am worrying about at this moment." We cannot curl up in a ball and have hope poured over us. Instead we must find hope in the solutions we ourselves have determined. Don't look for hope passively. Seek hope aggressively.

Hope means hoping when everything seems hopeless. G. K. Chesterton

It is no accident that above the entrance to Dante's Inferno of Hell is the inscription, *"Leave behind all hope, you who enter here."* Many reading this will have experienced a period of sheer, utter hopelessness at some moment in life: the absolutely failed relationship that does not offer a sliver of hope to be reconciled; the child who turns his back on your unconditional love and dives into a life of drug abuse and dissolute living; the intractable financial problem that offers no place to turn for a solution; a dreaded diagnosis of a terminal illness that leaves you panicky with fear; your most beloved

11

taken from you in an instant by a massive heart attack or a catastrophic accident.

These, and dozens of scenarios like them, can leave us teetering on the precipice of hell's yawning pit without a shred of hope. Consider that time in your own life when you experienced complete hopelessness. Most of us have been there, even if only for a moment or two. This is the time we need spiritual, not secular, hope to visit our broken spirit. Through our foreboding and fears we remind ourselves that God said He would never send us more than we can handle. We recall the words from the Talmud "...this, too, shall pass." In microscopic amounts, we introduce hope back into our souls. We listen to Chesterton tell us, "Hope means hoping when everything seems hopeless." We re-discover God's in-dwelling. "I thought You had abandoned me God. Now I've come to see that You were still there, all along. Thank You for sticking with me."

Man can live for about forty days without food, about three days without water, about eight minutes without air...but only for one second without hope. Hal Lindsey

Having just described some situations that seem hopeless, we also recognize that we can only survive in that state for an instant. We <u>must</u> believe there is a solution, a way out, a lifeline for any mess we're in. If we don't believe this, what then? Hopelessness is hell. A renewed sense of hope is ignited by trust in God. Let's face it: trust can be a difficult and elusive virtue. Trusting God to extricate us from a seemingly hopeless situation means we have to surrender ourselves totally and no longer rely upon our own abilities to solve a problem. And how some of us hate to lose control this way! So, here is our dilemma: trust is the key to hope but trust implies loss of control and most of us are uncomfortable letting go. Maybe our prayer should focus on receiving the gift of trust and learning how to surrender. With that virtue embedded in our soul, hope becomes more real and vibrant no matter what life circumstances we face. As Father Richard Berg, CSC has written in his excellent book, *Fragments of Hope – My Life As a Holy Cross Priest,* [3] "Hope is a gift for expectant living today. Eventually we realize that hope is a gift from God. It attracts our future into our life now. Hope is a gift bringing us strength from the future to help us now get through our inevitable challenges and fears."

We must expect finite disappointment, but never lose infinite hope. Martin Luther King Jr.

We cannot be Pollyanna about everything in life. The human condition means all will suffer some pain, anguish, difficulty and sorrow. Our human hope will probably wobble, stagger and, perhaps, come crashing down. Perfect trust in God and a well-developed virtue of hope will not combine to make life a perfect bowl of cherries all the time. As Dr. King said, we need to be prepared for the rough patches in life. They will surely come to all of us. Our hope is not human and finite; it is a gift to us from our Infinite Creator. As Mark Evans has written, "God can inject hope into an absolutely hopeless situation." So, we all know where we must turn when our soul is gasping for hope. We turn to God. As Great Pope John Paul II wrote, "I plead with you...never, ever give up on hope, never doubt, never tire and never become discouraged. Be not afraid." That may be a pretty high standard to live up to for those of us who are flawed and weak human beings. Remembering that God dwells in each of us makes this prayer easier for us to recite.

Hope is a waking dream. Aristotle

For each of us, then, hope exists in the background of our souls. We see it at work in the little events of our lives. Hope is not something we always dwell upon, but we exercise this virtue often. When faced with major challenges and difficulties, hope leaps to the front of our souls and we turn to God with trust that He will assist us in finding a pathway that leads us away from fear, anxiety and suffering. The following quote will sum up how most of us feel about the virtue of hope.

We ask God to increase our hope when it is small, awaken it when it is dormant, confirm it when it is wavering, strengthen it when it is weak and raise it up when it is overthrown. John Calvin.

This brief but profound prayer by Calvin is a perfect capstone to this chapter.

CHAPTER 3

HOW ARE MY FUNDAMENTALS: FAITH, HOPE AND LOVE?

LOVE

I cannot think of another word in the English language that is used with such liberal license as the word *love*. "I love my morning coffee." "Don't you just love this weather we are experiencing?" "I love my fresh fruit everyday...and it loves me, too." "I love that new movie; it is so realistic." Every day, we hear others use the word *love* this way and most of us are guilty of inexact usage, too. In our daily vernacular we often substitute the word *love* when we really mean we like, or appreciate, or admire some person, place, event or object. The casual use of the word *love* seems to depreciate its meaning when we <u>really</u> try to describe this important emotion. For our purposes, we define *love* as the intensely affectionate concern for the well being of another person. Well, that is mostly accurate, but we need some expansion of this definition.

When using the word *love* in relation to another person, or ourselves, we must be specific about the relationship. We observe six different types of love:

- <u>Maternal/Paternal love</u>. This is the type of love that a mother or father has for a child or grandchild.

15

- <u>Fraternal or Phileo love</u>. This is the love that siblings or close cousins experience and also extends to very dear personal friends who may not be related. This type of love is most often exhibited in a close friendship. Best friends will display this generous and affectionate love for each other as each seeks to make the other happy[4]. It's also the love we need to feel toward our neighbor. Another name for this is *Brotherly* love. This type of love is not always easy to develop.

- <u>Eros love</u>. This is the love shared by people who experience a sexual relationship such as a married couple, a young couple headed toward a lifelong commitment to each other or other non-related people who are physically attracted to each other.

- <u>Love of God</u>. Because we cannot feel or touch God, the love we have for Our Creator is based on a strong sense of gratitude, the peace and hope we experience from God's presence in our lives and the goodness that seems to flow to us from God. Sacred scripture makes reference to *Agape* love which is of and from God, whose very nature is love itself. It comes to us without any strings attached. He loves us not because we deserve to be loved, but because it is His nature to love us[5]. Agape love is abundantly available especially to those who think of themselves as unloved and unlovable.

- <u>Charity</u>. This subtle distinction in love refers to generous actions or the willingness to give to those in need. It also emphasizes loving elements of kindness, consideration for others, humanity and empathy.

- Love of Self. In sacred scripture, we are told to "...love our neighbors as ourselves." This can be a real problem for some people. A lot of us don't love ourselves very much. We only see our imperfections, faults and failings. Many folks gazing inward do not see a person who is loved. This is often deeply rooted in early childhood. The feeling spawns frustration and resentment and makes us unable to forgive others.[6] If we struggle with self-love it is often hard for us to visualize ourselves as loved by God or by another person. Of course, none of us are perfect. We are all flawed human creatures. But, we must never forget that God loves us individually and unconditionally *just the way we are.* If God is willing and happy to love us, warts and all, it would be a sin of pride for us not to love ourselves in the same way. Hoping to experience love to the fullest, we must convince ourselves that our imperfect body and soul still merits God's infinite and everlasting love. If God thinks we are that lovable, can't we at least do the same?

So, we begin our examination of love by asking ourselves a series of questions. Do I find myself to be lovable? Am I loved? Who are the people in my life for whom I feel a true sense of love? Can I identify people that cause me to feel an opposite emotion to love, that is, hatred? If so, what has caused me to withhold all love from those people? Do I believe that God loves me unconditionally and dwells within me even though I may have turned my back to God because of my sinfulness? Most humans will experience some difficulty with love during the course of their lives. That fact does not give us permission to give up on love.

The opposite of love is not hate, it is indifference.
Elie Wiesel

The question is posed above...whom do I hate? Mr. Wiesel, the great chronicler of the Holocaust, says indifference, not hate, juxtaposes love. Many of us feel uncomfortable admitting we hate another person. Hate seems such a vicious, violent and vile emotion. It is much easier to turn your back on someone you intensely dislike, to treat them with haughty disdain, to act as if they don't exist. Which is worse? Hate implies we hope the very worst happens to another. This is bad enough, surely, but is it worse than treating someone as if they are invisible and feeling no interest in them one way or another? Ask yourself: Have you ever been totally ignored, excluded or marginalized by another? Have you done the same thing to someone else especially a person who was entitled to or deserved your love? How did you feel when treated this way? How do you think the other person felt when you treated them in this way? We need to eliminate both hate and indifference from our emotional lexicon. God has told us quite clearly to do that

"How do you spell 'love,'" asked Piglet. "You don't spell it, you feel it," said Pooh.
A. A. Milne, *Winnie-the-Pooh*

We can spend a lot of time defining love. The distinctions between different types of love can be carefully studied. We have already tried to accomplish this in the introduction to this segment of the book. But, as lovable Winnie-the-Pooh simply said about love, "...you feel it." That's true for most of us. In our interaction with family, friends, neighbors—or our God— we seldom concern ourselves with parsing words or artfully defining our emotions...we just feel it. And that may turn out to be the best way for us to measure both the depth and breadth of our love.

We accept the love we think we deserve.
Stephen Chbosky

We have all seen the athletes pounding their chests in self-adulation after making a great play in a stadium full of rabid fans. In less public venues, an acquaintance will regale us with stories about their business prowess or some other success they have achieved in their private lives. We think to ourselves, "Wow! Those people must really have a high personal opinion of themselves." That is often true. However, most of us also know someone who turns down jobs and avoids getting involved by saying, "I don't have any skill or talents and I louse up most things I do; you don't want me around screwing things up." Instead of chest pounding and braggadocio, we are dealing with someone who undervalues himself or herself. Frequently, we may actually be observing someone afflicted with self-loathing. Face it; loving someone else will be pretty hard if we cannot visualize ourselves as lovable. This belief which almost always follows the feeling that we are not loved results because we feel some terrible defect that makes us unlovable and unworthy of love now or in the future.[5]

We must assume the mindset that God doesn't make junk. He made each of us in His own image and likeness; that seems like a pretty good start to me. Sure, we have fears, weaknesses, faults and human defects. Remember, God loves you unconditionally in spite of these. We must overcome the feeling that we don't deserve love; we do! And that begins with loving yourself.

Most of us are more lovable than we think we are. Get used to it! As Gautama Buddha has written, "You yourself, as much as anybody in the entire universe, deserve your love and affection."

Love is not an affectionate feeling but a steady wish for the loved person's ultimate good as far as it can be obtained. C. S. Lewis

I have a slight quibble with this quote. I contend that love *may* be an affectionate feeling but certainly doesn't have to be. Hopefully, affection accompanies the love we feel toward mother and father, child or grandchild, siblings, other close family members and dear friends. We have all heard of...perhaps experienced...animosity between family members that can cause wrenching discord. Almost all of us may have someone in our extended family circle that we love—according to the C. S. Lewis quote—but don't necessarily like very much. Let us now project the idea of love to our neighbors in the local community, our nation and even the entire world. As previously noted God-made-Man told all of us to "Love your neighbor as yourself" and again, "Love one another as I have loved you." Even during the time of Christ people tried to wiggle out of this requirement by trying to keep the definition of "neighbor" as restrictive as possible. Jesus didn't fall for that line of reasoning. It was clear that he meant *everyone* when he spoke about our neighbor...everyone without exception.

The Bible tells us to love our neighbors and also to love our enemies, probably because they generally are the same people. G. K. Chesterton

We stipulate that loving someone half way across the world possessing different values and culture, who doesn't speak our language, worships a different god and may actually hate us, is no easy assignment. Yet we are called to embrace the concept that all people are blessed with ultimate goodness, even those folks we don't know, may not like and who may not like us either. Visualize what the world might be like if the idea of "love your neighbor" took hold. Our local community, nation and the world would look and act much differently. As Fr. Greg Boyle, S.J. writes, "We have grown accustomed to think that loving as God does is hard. We think it's about moral strain and obligation. We presume it requires a spiritual muscularity of which we are not capable, a layering of burden on top of sacrifice, with a side order of guilt. But, it was love, after all, that made the cross salvific, not the sheer torture of it."[7] Maybe the idea is worthwhile, you say, but it will never happen. The longest journey starts with a single step. What if you took the first step toward loving your neighbor? Do you think you might make a difference? Why don't you try and see?

If you judge people, you have no time to love them.
Mother Teresa

A major impediment to love is our own judgmentalism. Only the most sainted among us have not fallen prey to this character defect. We eagerly view others through our own prism of what is correct, authentic, proper and acceptable behavior. Should we observe someone doing or saying something we find unacceptable, it is a human tendency to consider that person with disapproval, question their motivation and judgment or even exhibit cynical disdain. Some of us are quick to mount our high horses and from that lofty perch look down our long, regal noses at any one who might express an opinion or take some action we disagree with. Perhaps I am being over-dramatic. I do believe that judging others by our own standards can inhibit love. People everywhere are different; each one we meet is unique. Why is it necessary for us to judge them? Can't we just accept them for who they are and recognize that God loves them unconditionally just as He does us? I am not in a position to preach to you; judging others is one of my finely honed talents. But, as Mother Teresa said, we shouldn't waste our energy judging others. It only uses up the time we have to learn to love them. Let us all leave the judging of others to God.

Love cannot be forced, love cannot be coaxed and teased. It comes out of heaven, unasked and unsought. Pearl S. Buck

At bedrock, love is an emotional response. We can work hard to develop the habit of loving others by showing genuine concern for their wellbeing. We can practice not being judgmental. In the final analysis, we need God's supporting grace to love others. How many of us pray frequently to be better lovers of our fellow men and women? As Mrs. Buck states, love may come to some of us unasked and unsought. Most of us need a little help, I think. Consider adding this petition to your daily prayer: Dear God, give me the grace to love better and show me how to extend this love to all my neighbors in my family, in my community and in the world. Amen.

Who, being loved, is poor? Oscar Wilde

Think about this: Knowing that someone loves you provides you with a warm and comfortable feeling. The words we hear from someone may not always be exactly "I love you" since that expression isn't appropriate in every social setting. But even a hearty greeting with a sincere smile, a gentle hug, the statement, "Gee, you're terrific" or "I feel so blessed to have you in my life," lets us know that we are loved. Hearing those words can do wonders for you. If you do the same type of thing to someone else, can't you imagine that they might feel great, too? So whether we are the one loved or the one giving love to someone else, all parties to this social transaction are richer for the experience. As Mr. Wilde said, "Who, being loved, is poor?" Consider how you might make someone richer today by showing them your love. Perhaps someone will do the same favor for you.

Love is how you stay alive even after you're gone.
Mitch Albom

Think back, remembering close family members and dear friends whose earthly lives have ended. It might be many years since some loved ones departed but we still have vivid memories of them. Those recollections may include regret or guilt ("I wish I had stayed in closer contact"), respect and admiration ("What wonderful and productive lives they lived") but, most of all, we remember the love we shared with them. We fondly recall the gentle way they dealt with us, the encouragement and support they provided and the unconditional love they gave even when we messed up something in our lives. They lived a life of love, spoke their love to us and showed by their actions how much they loved us. As Mr. Albom says, love is how they stay alive in our hearts. How about you? Will there be a group of people who will remember you and your loving ways long after you are gone? If you have some doubts, what can you do now to amend your life to become more loving to others?

The greatest thing to remember is that though our feelings come and go, God's love for us does not.
C. S. Lewis

We can read all the books in the world, drop to our knees in frequent prayer but in spite of all our good intentions, we will find ourselves in periods where we don't feel too loving towards others. A family member wounds us, a friend abuses our trust, someone in our community cheats us and around the world a so-called "neighbor" kills a child in the name of religion. I don't feel very loving towards all these people I have been called upon to love. Our Constant God has no such problem with love. He continues to love us all—you and me—even when we fail to follow His commands to "love one another as I have loved you." We decide not to love; He never stops loving. We give up on family, friends and neighbors near and far; not so God, He is lovingly persistent.   Sometimes our very best prayer may be: "God I can't love this person right now. Will you please love him or her for me until I can get back on track?" I am absolutely positive God will answer that prayer affirmatively. When you need some temporary help in loving others, turn to your God.

...faith, hope and love remain, these three; but the greatest of these is love. First Letter of St. Paul to the Corinthians, Chapter 13, Verse 13

We sum up this section with a quote from Paulo Coelho:

"Love simply is."

CHAPTER 4

HAVE I FORGIVEN EVERYONE WHO HAS WOUNDED ME?

Of all the virtues, forgiveness may be the most difficult for us humans. Out of the blue, someone says or does something we find to be personally insulting or offensive. Our reaction may be instant or delayed. We may feel and display an immediate burst of fury or hurt accompanied by strong, direct and angry language. Worse perhaps, we may exhibit a delayed but deep and dark sense of brooding resentment at the alleged offense visited upon us. Often the wound is more severe if delivered to us by someone we are close to—a family member or a dear friend. No matter how it happens we have a score to settle and some of us won't be happy until we receive an abject apology from a chastened offender or until some type of comparable pain is meted out to the person who has offended us.

The prior paragraph paints us as pretty nasty people. I'm sorry about that...perhaps you are not like that at all. Unfortunately, our reaction to some personal offenses may be uncomfortably similar to what is described. Let us stop here for a quick examination of our own consciences. Think about the one area of your life that causes you the most spiritual difficulty. I will be surprised if the answer—when honestly examined—is not forgiveness of others. Perhaps this is merely a self-confession and does not apply to you at all. If true, please accept my sincere apology. I know it is a serious problem for me and I believe it may be for you, too. If I am wrong, you have my permission to skip this section of my book.

> *People in general would rather die than forgive. It's THAT hard. If God said, in plain language, "I'm going to give you a choice; forgive or die", a lot of people would go ahead and immediately order their coffin.* Sue Monk Kidd

Isn't that sad? Unfortunately, it is also true. For some reason, a lot of us seem to revel in nurturing hurts instead of forgiving them and moving on. Why don't we just say to the person who offended us, "I was really hurt by what you said. I'm sure you didn't mean to offend me. While I was wounded by that, I want you to know that I forgive you because I really want to be reconciled with you." That sounds simple, doesn't it? As most of us know, that is the hardest statement to make in the whole world. Trying to get those words out can be extremely difficult for many of us. I can't tell you why. I just know it is. When something is hard for us to do, what is the best approach? Practice, practice, practice. Let's all practice forgiveness; maybe we will get better at it.

> *To forgive is to set a prisoner free and discover the prisoner was you*. Lewis B. Smedes

The first reaction is to think the person who has been forgiven by another is the major beneficiary in this social transaction. Not true. When we forgive someone for a hurt they have visited on us, we are the principal benefactors. As Mr. Smedes says, those of us holding on to hurts and grievances find we are set free by a willing and sincere offer of forgiveness to the person we hold responsible for our pain. At this moment, what person in your life is holding you prisoner because you won't forgive him or her? Isn't it time to change?

The weak can never forgive. Forgiveness is the attribute of the strong. Mohandas K. Ghandi

Standing up for my rights and stubbornly demanding apologies shows the strength of my character, right? Not according the great Indian spiritual leader. He correctly argues that the weak find forgiveness to be difficult. Only those of strong character are able to forgive those who have offended them. When you find forgiveness the hardest thing to give, remind yourself that God's grace offers you the ability to be strong and forgive.

To be a true Christian means to forgive the inexcusable because God has forgiven the inexcusable in you. C. S. Lewis

Ah, we now get to the heart of the matter. As we daily say the Lord's Prayer, "...forgive us our trespasses as we forgive those who trespass against us," we are eager to have God's mercy and forgiveness for our own sins but often find ourselves much less willing to be so forgiving to others. Sorry...we can't have it both ways. The Lord has told us that we must be willing to forgive others in the same way we have been forgiven. There are no loopholes here. It's perfectly alright to admit we need a lot of God's graces to be forgiving of others. He has told us to ask Him for these graces; He will give them to us as needed.

Forgiveness is not about forgetting. It is about letting go of another person's throat.
William Paul Young

In his wonderful book, "The Shack," Mr. Young tells a semi-fictional tale about the murder of his young daughter at the hands of a vicious predator. A feeling of deep and malevolent hatred eventually turns into a sense of forgiveness through the intervention of the Holy Trinity portrayed by a most unlikely trio of characters. The principal theme of the book—a run-a-way bestseller—was forgiveness and redemption.[8] Mr. Young described that he had to first let go of the offender's throat before he could take the next step of forgiveness. His experience may be like ours. Forgiveness may not come in one step but may develop over a series of steps. That's okay. Final forgiveness is the goal and if that happens like peeling layers of an onion, that's alright. Do you have anyone's throat in your hands? Start the forgiveness process by letting go. After awhile, with God's grace, we may get to the point where complete forgiveness has taken place.

People are often unreasonable and self-centered. Forgive them anyway. Mother Teresa

Sometimes the one offending us turns out to be a mean-spirited, self-absorbed, first-class jerk. Being hurt by a snarky person gives us a wonderful rationale for not forgiving the offense. Justifying ourselves we may say, "Just look at the source of that nasty insult that was just thrust on me! Why would I even think of forgiving that person? He has a history of hurling this kind of invective at everyone...he doesn't deserve my forgiveness." We find it very easy to hold on to our anger and harden our resolve not to forgive. When we take this position, the suggestion of Mother Teresa is very hard to accomplish. Even those who seem least deserving of forgiveness require us to do so. That is what God calls us to do.

We don't forgive people because they deserve it. We forgive them because they need it, because we need it. Bree Despain

Ms. Despain offers a slightly different perspective from Mother Teresa. Here we are called to forgive people when they are undeserving — especially when they are undeserving — because they need the forgiveness. More importantly, we need to forgive them to free us from being a prisoner to our own anger and hurt. The more we think about forgiveness it becomes apparent why this is a difficult virtue. But nothing is impossible for God. We turn to Him saying, "Lord, I know you have forgiven me; let me forgive others in like manner."

Forgiveness is not an occasional act, it is a constant attitude. Martin Luther King, Jr.

Most of us will think of forgiveness as a discreet act in response to a specific hurtful event. We understand that we are called to forgive; we will do so (hopefully) when we have been offended. But Rev. King says this is not really the case. He contends that we must have a consistent forgiving spirit at all times. Instead of waiting to forgive until we are hurt, Dr. King tells us that forgiveness must be a part of our psychological makeup. In other words, we are always prepared to forgive even before we experience some specific pain. Would that be easy for you to incorporate in your spiritual profile? Honestly, it would be difficult for me.

***It is important that we forgive ourselves for making
mistakes. We need to learn from our errors and
move on****. Steve Maraboli

When thinking of forgiveness we almost always
project that outwards towards some other person. We
may need to think of this is a different way. Yes, we
must forgive others who have somehow offended us. As
important, we must we willing and able to forgive
ourselves for our own mistakes and offenses committed
upon others. In many situations, the lack of self-love
may be caused because we have not forgiven ourselves
for the stupid things we may have done. When praying
for the grace of forgiveness, remember yourself.

***An eye for an eye and the whole world would be
blind****. Kahlil Gibran

In the Old Testament scriptures we hear of
commensurate vengeance committed on an offending
party. Yes, if we lose an eye because of the negligence of
another, we must seek to inflict the same punishment
on the offending party. What folly this is, says Gibran. If
we are only satisfied with hurting those who offend us
with an equal measure of pain we are playing a foolish
zero sum game. As Gibran said, if the metaphor of "an
eye for an eye" is the standard by which we deal with
others, the whole world will soon be blind. Instead of
equal pain, we must adopt the principle that our
forgiveness is given without strings attached. I forgive
you; you don't have to do anything to make it up to me.
While this may be the most difficult type of forgiveness
we are called to offer, it is what God asks of us. You and
I can follow God's calling in this regard if we consistently
ask for God's grace to forgive.

The practice of forgiveness is our most important contribution to the healing of the world.
Marianne Williamson

Think about this. If individual family members practiced forgiveness towards their relatives, if contentious community factions were willing to forgive and forget, if nations stepped away from conflict and said let's be good neighbors to each other—how would this change our world? Is this an idealistic dream? Perhaps. But what if you started the process by contacting that estranged family member or neighbor with whom you had a simmering feud and said, "You have hurt me in the past but I forgive you and I'm sorry if any of my actions may have offended you. Will you also forgive me, please?" Do you think anything might change for the better if you were able to get those twenty-nine words out of your mouth? I think it might be the beginning of a small but growing miracle. Yes, the practice of forgiveness may well be our most important contribution to the healing of the world. Are you willing to give it a try today?

Then Jesus said, "Father forgive them, they know not what they do."
Gospel of St. Luke, Chapter 23, Verse 34

The innocent Jesus Christ provides a perfect model for each of us as we try to be forgiving people. Hanging on the cross He pleads for his Father to forgive those who have so unjustly brutalized him. Can each of us do less than this when forgiveness is needed? But, this is not so easy for us. Let us all resolve to pray fervently, while gazing upon the crucifix, asking Jesus for the grace, courage and humility to be able to forgive as he forgave. It is only through his help that we can expect lead a life centered on forgiveness to others.

CHAPTER 5

HOW GENEROUS AM I WITH MY TIME, TALENT AND TREASURE?

Generosity is a greatly admired virtue. The generous person is known as one who gives abundantly and shares the valuable things he or she has with others who are in need. Being generous stresses gifts freely given, charitable care for those less fortunate and munificent bounty liberally shared with others. If only we all possessed the virtue of generosity! Alas, some folks are the opposite of generous; they are selfish, caring much more for themselves and forgetful of others. This is not a judgment, just a fact.

Most of us reflexively focus on money or wealth when we think about generosity. Giving financial gifts to a church, school, cause or charitable organization often represents the most obvious type of generosity. While money is a vital need, the giving of one's time and talent may also epitomize valuable gifts that can be shared.

In our fast-paced, frenetic world, time is often the most valuable commodity anyone has. To give time in the service of others may be the most important thing any of us can do to assist a church or community organization that provides support or service. And what about our talents? Many of us have special skills that can be most helpful to schools or charities. Think about things like in-depth computer knowledge, financial planning or accounting expertise, medical or dental proficiency, organizational aptitude, vehicle repair competence and other skills. Our generosity with our time or talent may not require accumulated wealth or riches but could turn out to be even more valuable than money.

Each of us needs to check our own record about generosity. Have we been outward looking and generous or inward looking and selfish? Do we contribute money out of our abundance or out of our need? Have we set aside some of our valuable time to give in service to others or is every minute used up just for ourselves? Are our special talents, gifts from God, ever shared with those who could use our skills?

GENEROSITY

You give but a little when you give of your possessions. It is when you give of yourself that you truly give. Kahlil Gibran

Some people have been accused of being "checkbook Christians." That moniker implies that they may be happy to assuage their consciences by writing a check to charity but they never really want to get personally involved. It is easy to see how this can be true. People who need our help aren't always pleasant individuals. In fact, it may be downright unpleasant to be around them. While we should not judge those who give generously of their wealth to worthwhile causes, there is perhaps an even higher standard of generosity. The quote from Gibran does add context to our giving.

You have not lived fully today until you have done something for someone who can never repay you. John Bunyan

In today's world we often hear, "What's in it for me?" Many expect that their generosity will be repaid in one form or another such as a significant tax deduction, a glowing write-up in a local publication or some other type of acclaim for the generosity shown. There is nothing wrong with lowered taxes or accolades, but they may diminish one's gift if they represent the main purpose of giving. As Bunyan says, it is much better that we are generous without the thought of what we might get in return. It may be helpful to examine our reasons for giving. What is our expectation? Are we looking for praise or adulation? Have we been generous because it looked like the proper thing to do? Will we feel satisfied with our gift even if it is given anonymously and not acknowledged? Do we require thanks from those we gift?

"...For it is in giving that we receive."
St. Francis of Assisi

The great Saint Francis expresses the essence of generosity. Many have already experienced this reaction: When we give generously from the depths of our being, we feel a sense of uplifting satisfaction that warms our souls. This emotion seems more valuable than the value of any gift we may have given. As Francis says, we receive when we give.

When it comes to giving, some people stop at nothing. Vernon McLellan

This is a very tricky issue. None of us can judge the actions of another, especially those folks who do not give anything to charity. There can be good and valued reasons for not being charitable; all of us can think of a number of circumstances that prevent giving. We need to check ourselves first. Are we capable of giving? Are there any constraints upon our ability to give? Have we failed to share our gifts with the less fortunate? Do we give only what is left over? Do we give cheerfully or out of a sullen sense of duty? Do we believe that everything we have...everything...is a gift from God? Does your practice of giving honor the gifts that have been given freely to you? We must ask ourselves some tough questions.

You cannot do a kindness too soon because you never know how soon it will be too late.
Ralph Waldo Emerson

Many of us are procrastinators. We have good intentions but just don't follow through. This may lead to a guilty feeling when we miss the opportunity to help someone in need. We may need a wake-up call about our generosity. Don't wait! When we say we are going to do something charitable like writing a check or volunteering time we need to do it...now. As Emerson reminds us, don't delay being generous. By the time you finally get around to it, it may be too late.

TIME

Time is a created thing. To say, "I don't have time," is like saying, "I don't want to." Lao Tzu

There is another old saying: "If you don't want to do something, almost any excuse will do." The Chinese philosopher adds a further dimension. All of us feel starved for time at points in our lives. We have good intentions about doing a lot of things but then find we don't have time available to complete our plans. How often have we heard, "You will make time for things that are really important." It is disingenuous for us to say, "I would really like to volunteer my time to help out but I don't have any available." Don't you think you might find some time for something you determined was very worthwhile? Are you really saying, "I just don't want to," when you state no time exists? This is another good opportunity for each of us to check our motives.

Time is what we want most but what we use worst.
William Penn

Whether you are king or commoner, a millionaire or a pauper, every day of your life consists of eighty-six thousand four hundred seconds. No one gets one instant more or less. While living a harried existence, many will say "...if I only had more time!" Between our jobs, families, shopping, social commitments and dozens of other activities we arrive at the end of most days exhausted. The "to do" list for tomorrow looks even longer than the one we didn't nearly complete today. It's a fact that some of us are like derelict old boats—we leak time like the boat leaks water. Just think of the time that evaporates each day on minor or meaningless tasks. We check our social media sites endlessly for the latest text message, Tweet or Instagram. We sit at our computer playing Solitaire. Time is spent parked in front of the television watching re-runs of old comedy shows. Long periods are spent on the phone speaking to someone we will see face-to-face tomorrow. We duplicate errands to the same shopping center on the same day. Here's the point: most of us are guilty of wasting a lot of time. Think about your own habits. Couldn't you find significant chunks of time in your daily routine *if you really wanted to?* Let's make a real effort to find those minutes that can be given to worthwhile activities like helping others in our community. We can do it if we try.

Yesterday is gone. Tomorrow has not yet come. We have only today. Let us begin. Mother Teresa

How often we lose sight of this basic truth! The past is gone; there is absolutely nothing we can do to change it. The future is exactly that; we can deal with it when it arrives. All we have is now, this moment, the present. Let's all quit worrying about what might have been or what might be in the future. We need to focus on the encounter we are now having, the prayer we are making, the good work we are trying to accomplish. As Mother Teresa tells us, quit worrying about what is in our rear view mirror or what is around the next bend of the road. Let's get busy right now while we are in this moment.

It's a shame to waste time. We always think we have so much of it. Mitch Albom

Old is defined as ten years older than you are right now. Most of us see the end of our own earthly existence as an indistinct horizon far away. There is always more time to do all the things we want to do and know we should do. Yes, there is plenty of time—until there isn't. This is not about some shadowy figure in a black, hooded robe carrying a scythe following us down the road. We are merely reminded that all the time we all have will finally be used up. Hopefully, we do the things that are important before we reach the end of our earthly presence here. What are your plans to accomplish that goal?

TALENT

Our talents are the gifts God gives to us. What we make of our talents is our gift back to God.
Leo Buscaglia

Every single person has a unique charism. No matter how modest, God has bestowed gifts on each of us. My personal mantra is, "I have never met a person who is not superior to me in some way." I absolutely believe that. God has been generous to each of us and none is bereft of some gift or talent. It is our obligation to develop these gifts that have been loaned to us. We are not required to do great things, but we are called to do small things in a great way. When we do our best with the gifts God has given us we are preparing a gift to give back to our God. Do you agree that you have some requirement to thank God for all he has given to you?

Life is entrusted to a man as a treasure, which must not be squandered, as a talent, which must be used well. Great Pope John Paul II

God has given every person many gifts, the greatest of which is life itself. We exist only because our Creator wills that it be so. A gift so enormous demands that we employ it in beneficial and effective ways. How do I, a weak and flawed human being, use this basic yet colossal endowment in ways that give glory to my Creator? God is not looking for supermen or superwomen. He wants us to do our best with what He has given us. He looks to our effort, not necessarily our success. As Pope John Paul II says, we must try not to squander our gifts but use our talents as best we can. How are you doing in this regard?

When I stand before God at the end of my life, I would hope that I would not have a single bit of talent left, and I could say, "I used everything you gave me." Erma Bomback

I find this to be a simple yet compelling prayer. When we breathe our final earthly breath, wouldn't it be wonderful to say, "Lord, I didn't hold anything back. Every single gift you loaned me and all the graces I was given were used to build up your Kingdom. I wasn't always successful, but I tried as hard as I could." How do you think Jesus might respond to this prayer? I think he might say, "Well done, good and faithful servant. Now come and occupy the place I have prepared for you." Starting right now, let's pledge to use all the talent, gifts and graces God gives us for his greater glory.

Most people overestimate others' talents and underestimate their own. Orrin Woodward

"Give that assignment to George. He has amazing skill," we say. When the next task comes along we say, "I don't have the ability to do that; find someone else." Most of us are quick to overestimate the abilities of others and don't think too highly of our own talents. Often this turns out to be false humility. We undervalue ourselves because we have not yet accepted the fact that God has given us many unique gifts. We also lack confidence in our abilities and are afraid we might embarrass ourselves if we try something and fail. Just take a look at Moses or Jonah. God will not necessarily check us for our success, but He will judge us on our efforts. Each of us must make an objective inventory of the talents and skills. Next, we must each decide that God has endowed us with these talents for a reason. Finally, we must be willing to use these skills to the best of our human ability, always asking God to give us the grace to use these gifts wisely and effectively. Have you taken a personal skills inventory yet? How do you think you might use these God-given gifts to give honor to God's plan for you? Each one of us has unique talent and God expects us to use that to better our world.

TREASURE

What we spend, we lose. What we keep will be left for others. What we give away will be ours forever.
David McGee

Truly the use of money can be the root of all evil. As a friend once told me, there seems to be a direct link between our heart and our wallet. Of all the things we want to control, money is probably our top priority. Some of us fail to give generously because we are concerned there will not be enough left over for our own needs. We hold back our gifts when the future looks uncertain and we worry our wealth will evaporate. Take on the job as a fund-raising chair for a church or school—you will then know what I am talking about. Often, the most affluent have a difficult time parting with their money. There are so many clichés about money; they won't be repeated here. We are called to examine our basic beliefs about money and our motives for giving—or failing to do so. We know that it is impossible for any of us to be more generous than God. Can't we each figure out a way to be prudent with our money as well as generous? Do you give to charity out of your need or your plenty? Is charitable giving the first check you write each month or the last? Do you have an appreciation for where your wealth has come from? Let us each work to be just slightly more generous than our comfort level for giving. This is a worthwhile target.

The Book of Sirach (Ecclesiasticus)
Chapter 35, Verses 8-9

These scriptures verses tell all to show a cheerful countenance when making our contributions and to pay our tithes in a spirit of joy. We are also advised to give to the Most High as He has given to us, that is, generously. We ask for the grace and fortitude, dear God, to fulfill these holy admonitions in our own daily lives.

CHAPTER 6

HOW ABOUT MY SPIRITUAL LIFE AND PERSONAL PRAYER?

All of us possess both a body and a soul, at least according to most philosophy and religious belief. Our finite human bodies exist in a physical world constrained by time, space and physical laws. In the normal course of events, a body is born, grows, matures and starts to fade as the years pass. Eventually it dies and returns a handful of chemicals, proteins and bones to the earth. Inexorably linked to the human body is the spiritual soul that we cannot touch or see or feel. While some disagree or question, most believe the soul has an infinite life, living on forever after the body has died. It is impossible to summarize the entire understanding of Plato, Aristotle, Thomas Aquinas and all the great philosophical and religious intellectuals in a single paragraph. But this is the essence: The human being is comprised of a human body, an intellect and an infinite soul. This is what distinguishes the human being from all other creatures in the known universe. For the purposes of this book, we stipulate that this is so.

Few of us wake up each morning to contemplate deeply how our body, intellect and soul are co-existing to form us as a human being. Most will compartmentalize these three elements, dealing with them separately even though they are wondrously and seamlessly integrated. The body and its needs often assume priority. We all require rest, nourishment, physical and other activity;

43

those items must be dealt with on a current basis. Meanwhile, in the background our mind is racing, planning for the day ahead, dealing with problems that must be solved and creating activity scenarios that we believe will be in our best interest. Our soul (indistinguishable from the intellect?) is the constant connection to the infinite, the spiritual side of our being. It is playing an important part of our existence by helping us to distinguish right from wrong, good from evil and permitting us to contemplate our relationship with the Great Supreme Spirit...whom we call God. Unfortunately, our bodily and intellectual pursuits can become so distracting that we may fail to focus on our spiritual side much if at all. We can actually lose a complete dimension of who we are.

This chapter deals with how to nourish our souls and the need to develop the spiritual dimension of our existence. Future chapters will consider how to care properly for our bodies—with our obligation to do so— and how we need to cultivate our intellectual side as well. In these next few pages we will review the state of our spiritual life, personal piety and our prayer life.

What lies behind us and what lies before us are tiny matters compared to what lies within us.
Ralph Waldo Emerson

Too many of us fret about our past spiritual mistakes or worry about how we can possibly lead better lives in the future. Intellectually all of us know the past is over and done with—it cannot be changed. The future is not yet here; we will deal with that when it comes. What is really important is what lies within us at this moment. Only in the present can we reach out to our God and establish a loving relationship. Only in the present can we reach the conclusion that God dwells within us. Only in the present can we snuggle in the enfolding arms of our loving God. The past is history; the future is over the horizon. Live your spiritual life in this moment. Let God know you love Him now.

Our efforts will never be sufficient on their own. Only the grace of Christ can will us the victory.
Jacques Philippe

Over time, many of us will be inspired by a retreat, a spiritual book or a Lenten season to re-energize our spiritual lives. We conclude that we have become slack or lazy letting our relationship with God assume a secondary role in our day-to-day existence. We resolve to do a better job with our prayer, participate more actively in sacramental life and live our lives more in sync with God's commands. If this new-found resolve fails, it is often because we tried to reform based solely on our own human strength and failed to turn humbly to the Lord for his help. Remember, we cannot even love Him more unless He gives us the grace to do so.

I think the reason we sometimes have this false sense that God is so far away is because that is where we have put Him. When we are in need and call on Him in prayer, we wonder where He is. He is exactly where we left Him. Ravi Zacharias

Although we cannot see God, all of us create images of what He looks like and where His heavenly home is. The first person of the Trinity is often thought of as a father figure seated on a large throne in heaven that we visualize "up there" in some distant place in the universe or beyond. Our finite intellects place God in a mighty and remote location because we cannot visualize how such an Infinite Spirit could be anyplace else. How wrong we are to think that way! Jesus, the second person of the Trinity, told His disciples, "The Father and I will come and dwell within you." Yes, God—Father, Son and Spirit—lives within each of us providing love, comfort, encouragement and support. Some of us may reject this indwelling of God because of hardened hearts or disbelief that God could actually love someone as weak and wretched as we may be. But, God does not give up. He is always present within us, reaching out with love. We need only respond. God is not distant; He is here within us.

Pray always. Pray all ways.
Tom Tomaszek, The Five Loaves Ministry

Tom offers two brief sentences both with similar words but conveying completely different concepts. Scripture tells us, "Pray without ceasing." All but the greatest mystics or the most remote hermits have a difficult time praying constantly. Human cares frequently distract us throughout our days. We do our best, offering little prayers when we think to do so. Many will use human devices to serve as reminders. For example, some pray whenever they open a door; whenever they place their key in the car ignition; whenever they respond to a mobile phone call; when the hourly alarm on their smart phone goes off. Each of us can think of a hundred little things we do each day that could remind us to pray...even if for just a few seconds.

Second, we are told to pray all ways. Some do best with "formula" prayers or ones read out of a book. Others are comfortable with spontaneous prayer. Still others will receive inspiration from reading the Bible. The Rosary works for some folks. There are many ways to pray. We should try them all but concentrate on the methods that seem to work best for us. God hears every kind of prayer and answers our prayer...in His own way.

The value of consistent prayer is not that God will hear us but that we will hear Him. William McGill

Sometimes we think that consistent and persistent prayer is what is needed for God to hear us. As Mr. McGill points out, that is the wrong way for us to look at prayer. The more effectively we pray the better we are able to hear God's message for us and what He is calling us to do. It is often very difficult to understand, let alone hear, what God wishes us to do or be. The more consistent our prayer life is, the easier it will become to hear God's voice and discern what He is calling us to become in this life.

Prayer is the center of the Christian life. It is the only necessary thing. It is living with God in the here and now. Henri Nouwen

How can we have a deep relationship with anyone without speaking to him or her about our yearnings, hopes, difficulties and fears? Nouwen makes the case that prayer is the principal thing and center of the Christian life. Do you believe that to be so? If our prayer is the way we communicate with God on a regular basis, how are you keeping your end of the bargain? Intellectually, we know prayer gives us strength, courage and a feeling of relationship with God. Then why do we often fail to pray? It is a matter of priorities; we must cultivate a humble acceptance that we need God in our lives. Let us all strive to live with God in the here and now by developing a richer and more consistent prayer life.

If we do not feel like praying, then we should pray until we do feel like praying. Ezra Taft Benson

Yes, you say, I know I should spend more time in prayer. But, I often don't know what to say, I'm frequently distracted and, frankly, I just don't feel like praying. The great Mormon leader, Mr. Benson, offers a sure cure for our problem. All of us know that prayer can be difficult and it is often easier to do something else rather than pray. Especially in times when we feel very arid spiritually the only thing we may be able to do is pray for the grace to pray effectively. Keep that in mind the next time you don't feel like praying.

We should seek not so much to pray but to become prayer. St. Francis of Assisi

St. Francis prayed each morning that every act he would do that day would be offered up as an action for the greater glory of God. Francis tells us that we can make our life a prayer. Even the boring, mundane and routine things we do each day can be offered to build God's kingdom on earth. While we may not have prayers constantly on our lips we can still lift up to God every single act we perform. Sounds like good prayer to me. I think God would respond to me if my whole life, my actions and my total being were a prayer.

Most of my struggles in the Christian life circle around these two themes: Why God doesn't act the way I want Him to and why I don't act the way God wants me to. Prayer is the precise point where these two themes converge. Philip Yancey

That idea certainly resonates with me. Why, I wonder in frustration, doesn't God answer my prayers in the way I want them answered? On the other hand, why do I act so often in a way that is disobedient to God's commands to me? Yancey suggests this is the ultimate intersection for prayer. We need to ask for God's help...if it is His will, we plead that God will answer us. We also need to pray with a sense of humility that we need God's graces in order to live the life He calls us to lead.

Pray, hope and don't worry. Worry is useless. God is merciful and will hear your prayers. Padre Pio

The last thing we need is for our pray to cause us stress. Am I praying right? Are my prayers effective? Does God really hear my prayers? Am I praying enough? Padre Pio says that we should relax, rely on the virtue of hope and quit worrying. We all know that our worry doesn't change one thing, but we do it anyway. The saintly Padre says worry is a waste of time. Concentrate on the fact that God loves us, is very patient and work on convincing yourself that your prayer is being heard. Because it is. Remember, some time we are called to "wait on the Lord." Be patient; God will get back to you eventually.

Your prayer for someone may or may not change them. But, it will always change you.
Craig Groeschel

We often find ourselves praying for another person. That individual may be in distress or facing some intractable problem so we wind up interceding for that person directly with God. Perhaps your prayer asks for reconciliation because of a broken relationship. Mr. Groeschel rightly points out that our prayer may be effective in a different way from how we planned. While the person prayed for may not be changed or saved by our prayerful effort, the one who does the praying is always changed in some way. Think of instances where you have prayed for others. What has been the result of that prayer on them? What has been the result on you?

Dear Jesus, do something! Vladimir Nabokov

# # #

Could it be that this is both the shortest and most effective way to pray?

Those of us, advanced in age, who attended Catholic grammar schools as youngsters remember The Baltimore Catechism. One of the first entries in that book was the question, "What is prayer?" The answer that we all memorized was, "Prayer is the lifting up of our minds and hearts to God." These were simple and understandable words for 3rd and 4th graders but also timeless and perfectly descriptive even now. They seem to entirely sum up all we have been talking about in this chapter.

Prayer is an integral part of our spiritual life, but not the only element. We need to do our best to follow God's commands by living pious lives in accordance with sacred scripture and the teachings of the Church. We need to worship in community on a regular basis. If your church denomination honors a sacramental heritage, you need to participate in that sacramental life with commitment and belief. Piety, sacramental life and prayer: This is how we claim our heavenly inheritance when our human life is completed. How are you doing in this regard?

CHAPTER 7

HAVE I EDUCATED MYSELF AS AN ADULT CHRISTIAN?

Here is a sad fact: The last time most adult Christians received any formal moral or spiritual training was a religious education program, youth group or Confirmation class while in high school. Yes, there are the Sunday homilies explaining the meaning of sacred scripture as it applies to our daily lives. Some of us may have attended a retreat or day of recollection along the way but those are often more inspirational than educational. Unless we have proactively sought religious education through books, periodicals or adult classes at our parish church, most of us are woefully lacking in the history of the Church or the Christian perspective on many issues being faced today. For some of us that means thirty, forty, even fifty years or more since we seriously studied our church's position on very significant moral and ethical questions being faced today by Christians throughout the world. Indeed, this is troubling.

Each of us must ask ourselves: Are we sufficiently informed to forcefully and effectively argue the Christian position on a number of relevant issues? For example: Why is stem cell research immoral? What is the First Amendment threat to the Church caused by the contraceptive mandate of the Affordable Care Act? Why does same-sex marriage undermine the fundamental social unit, a family composed of a mother and a father?

Why is the death penalty wrong? Why is abortion gravely immoral? What does the Preferential Option for the Poor really mean? These issues represent just a few of the major controversies faced by the Church and its adherents. Have we adequately educated and informed ourselves about these pressing social issues? Could we stand up in an open meeting and defend our Church and its teaching against a committed secular adversary? Or have we abjectly surrendered and been silenced by the pop cultural slogans about pro-choice, marriage equality, homophobia and extremist positions outside the mainstream of current social or political thought? It is distressing to note that the majority of Christians, especially Roman Catholics, have voted for political candidates in recent election cycles who consistently espouse positions starkly at odds with Christian principles, dogma and teaching. I do not suggest that church members should march in doctrinal lock step. Neither should they shun vigorous debate over moral, ethical and dogmatic issues. However, these debates cannot be effective unless those participating are educated and well informed about the topics being deliberated.

Is there any solution to this knowledge and education gap we face? We begin by acknowledging that none of us may become articulate spokespeople or renowned apologists for Christian theology and social positions espoused by our Church. But almost any of us can become effective and respected sources for reliable and credible information about Christian beliefs in our families and communities. Where do we first begin to educate ourselves? Most major dioceses publish a newspaper. Subscribe and read the paper thoroughly. There are dozens of national Christian periodicals that take various positions on social issues. Check them out and see which ones provide a theme that resonates with you. Viewpoints are not monolithic; make sure you examine all positions. Of course, church libraries and the Internet are replete with books and articles on Church history, the lives of the saints, Christian apologetics and positions on all religious matters. The complete Catechism of the Catholic Church is a fulsome statement of Christian belief and provides thorough background and reasoning on virtually every aspect of doctrine and dogma. Adult education classes in your parish or diocese can reinforce your knowledge. Attend them when you can. There are extensive resources for you to get your Christian education up to date. Take advantage of all you can. We need more Christian leaders and prophets. You can do your part to fill that urgent need. Ask God for the courage to be open-minded and thoroughly educated.

Education is the most powerful weapon which you can use to change the world. Nelson Mandela

I am quite sure Mr. Mandela had a secular context in mind when he made that statement. The idea also applies to our spiritual life and our participation in a Christian worship community. Just think of your own experiences: If you are well versed on a subject and can articulate your position, you often assume leadership of the conversation. Our churches need more people who have the facts and ideas to inspire others to action. You must discern if you have been called to step up to this leadership responsibility in your faith community. Do not be too easy on yourself when making this discernment.

Knowledge will give you the opportunity to make a difference. Claire Fagin

Knowledge may not guarantee that you will make a difference, but it will give you the opportunity. People everywhere seem confused and conflicted by all the different points of view presented on a range of issues. Nowhere is this more apparent than in religious congregations. What are we to believe? Is truth immutable or do we need to change with the times? How can I recognize false prophets in my midst? Knowledge can be faked...but not for long. The person who is genuinely informed and provides calm, reasoned information to his or her family, friends, co-religionists and to the community can truly make a difference. Knowledge, used for good, is like a rudder on a ship changing direction towards a more favorable port. This is the type of role to which we have been called by our God.

When we read and study the scriptures, benefits and blessings of many kinds come to us.
Howard W. Hunter

To be effective, informed Christians requires that we acquire knowledge from many sources. Sometimes in our search for the latest popular book or periodical we overlook the library of books, letters, essays and spiritual stories that is the bedrock of our religious conviction...the Bible. We Christians believe that every word of sacred scripture is the inspired work of the Holy Spirit and provides assistance to each person's salvation journey. Some of us may not be as familiar with the Bible as we should be. God's covenant with the Old Testament people and the wisdom of the prophets seamlessly leads us to the Incarnation, passion and death and Resurrection of God the Son. After the Ascension and Pentecost, we hear the stories of the struggles and growth of the fledgling Christian church.

One does not have to be a great Bible scholar to learn much. It is a story of faith, hope and love, especially the love of God for humankind. We are reminded that the truly educated Christian is deeply familiar with the Bible. How do you measure up to that call?

The mind is not a vessel to be filled, but a fire to be kindled. Plutarch

Education and knowledge are not ends unto themselves. You seldom change hearts by reciting facts in an uninspired way. If we decide to improve our spiritual knowledge we must not stop at facts; what we learn should fire our hearts with new love for our Almighty God and our neighbor. What good is mere knowledge? We must use that knowledge to help build God's kingdom here on earth. We are called to be the arms and legs of Jesus in the daily battle for souls. Do you accept that challenge?

Prayer without study is empty. Study without prayer is blind. Karl Barth

We have written previously about the importance and effectiveness of prayer. This chapter leads to a consideration of greater Christian knowledge and understanding about the major milestones on our personal salvation journey. Mr. Barth contends that a failure to integrate study along with prayer leads to imperfection in both. We add yet another element: effective Christian action. So the three—prayer, study and action—become the foundation of the active Christian life. Like a three-legged milking stool, should any of the three elements be missing, we will surely fall from our stool in an ignominious fashion. (Full credit is given to the Cursillo Movement for the milking stool concept). Please consider how you plan to integrate prayer, study and action into your daily life.

Only the educated are free. Epictetus

Without intellectual understanding we are captives to slogans and sound bites of information. How many times have you heard something like this: "I just don't understand some of the things my church does and why it opposes other policies that sound to me like a reasonable accommodation." Those uttering words like these probably haven't taken the time or effort to find the real answers to their own questions. This is not judgment but a plea that more of us make a serious attempt to improve our own spiritual education. As Epictetus says, only the educated are free. Don't you really aspire to that state of freedom?

Learning is not attained by chance; it must be sought for with ardor and attended to with diligence. Abigail Adams

We may wish for improved understanding through osmosis but all of us recognize education doesn't happen that way. Individually, we must decide that this is something important for our spiritual lives. As Mrs. Adams says, to increase our knowledge requires a level of passion and consistent diligence on our part. Our failure to commit to a path of improved spiritual education confines us to the captivity of slogans. We are also subject to others who may not have our best interests at heart. Are you willing to seriously promise yourself to be better informed about all things spiritual in the days, months and years ahead? Isn't this really what is in your best interest?

We can study until old age and still not finish.
Chinese Proverb

At what age can we relax and quit trying to learn more or understand more completely? There is no expiration date on our spiritual education. As this Proverb states we are never finished with this job. The most important question for us may be: When are we going to get started on this necessary component of spiritual living?

In the early centuries of the Christian Church, we had an educated group of clergy and religious; the common folks were expected to be pew sitting, dues paying sermon listeners. Those days are past history. Today the Church needs informed and engaged members who can effectively carry the Gospel message into the homes, schools, businesses and the public squares of communities everywhere. If you profess to be a Christian, a follower of Jesus Christ, you have taken this obligation directly upon yourself. You cannot fulfill this obligation without adequately educating yourself. Are you ready to start...now?

Greg Hadley

CHAPTER 8

HAVE I CREATED A LEGACY AND RECORDED MY STORY?

Recently there has been great interest in senior adults about creating an Ethical Will. This document can take many forms but the essential point is that the Will passes on the life values and important reflections of the author. Sometimes these Wills are lighthearted stories about experiences from early childhood right on through old age. Others may focus on collections of pictures with added commentary about who are in the photos, why the photos of people or places are significant and how the event helped to shape a life. Still others may be a series of short statements that summarize standards of moral and ethical principles one lived by. Whatever form the Ethical Will takes, it is a very significant document that helps shape future generations of descendants. It almost always turns out to contain spiritual values as well as human ones. Everyone approaching old age—or already there—should seriously consider producing his or her own Ethical Will...in writing.

These documents usually have very limited distribution; copies will be produced for the author's children, grandchildren and close family members. Most copies will be created on a copy machine at a local print shop but some have gone to elaborate lengths to have their Wills professionally produced in book form. Most authors probably hope their work will be discovered in a dusty attic box one hundred years from now. The Ethical Will is often most valuable to first and second-generation descendants. So few of us have much detailed information about our ancestors. Ask yourself: Do you know where your grandparents are buried? Where they were born? So much of this information is lost because it is not written down anywhere. So, all are encouraged to take the time to write down information about themselves while they are still able to do so.

Due to circumstances or ability, many will probably be unable to record all the information about themselves, commit their values to paper, or assemble any type of formal record of their life. This is understandable and we should not be critical of those who do not produce a written summary of their lives for their descendents. Whether recorded formally for posterity or merely a part of the memory of loved ones, we all do leave a legacy. We live on in the hearts of those who loved us while we're alive. They recall the advice we gave about difficult problems or how certain situations might be handled. One way or another, our spiritual and ethical values are conveyed and will be remembered by our families and descendants. Therefore, it becomes an important component of our spiritual journey to let future generation know how we felt, what we believed and the struggles we encountered in life. Written or passed on by word of mouth, our legacy will survive our passing from this world to the next. How would you like to be remembered? Have you let people know how you feel about life? Have you shared deeply your religious beliefs with others close to you? Our legacy is integral to our spiritual journey; that is why it is included in this book.

The greatest legacy you could ever leave your children or your loved ones: the history of how you felt. Simon Von Booy

Our legacy may include places we lived, schools we attended, where we worked, trips we took and describe our relationships with family, friends and loved ones. But, nothing is as important as the description of how we *felt*. How were we touched by the actions of others? What events affected our emotional and spiritual lives during our time on earth? The stories of our euphoric highs and devastating lows, the experiences of greatest loves, hurts, reconciliations, joyous times and painful losses—these are what really count. Some of us have a reserved nature that makes it difficult to share deeply our inmost feelings. Our legacy will lack significance unless we can overcome this natural reluctance to express how we really feel. In order to touch the spirits and souls of your descendents, you must work to find a new level of expression. "This is how I felt:" What a powerful statement!

No legacy is so rich as honesty. William Shakespeare

Some of us will avoid saying the whole truth or may shade facts just a little in order to protect others from any possible hurt or embarrassment. Consideration for the feelings of others is certainly commendable. Sometimes the greatest lessons are learned from unvarnished truth. While avoiding any judgmentalism or bitterness, our legacy must be based on complete honesty if it to be most effective. If we fail to share the tough parts of our lives, we wind up with a breezy narrative that may be interesting but not long remembered. Don't you wish you knew exactly how your ancestors felt about you even if some of those feelings were reminders of painful situations? As Shakespeare says, honesty is crucial.

> *Carve your name on hearts, not tombstones. A legacy is etched into the minds of others and the stories they share about you*. Shannon L. Alder

Whether your legacy is written or oral is not critically important. So long as your descendants have a clear memory of your values, beliefs and first principles of living a balanced human existence, then you have left them a valuable gift. Hopefully we will be remembered for the things we taught our children, grandkids, nieces and nephews or students in our charge. Wouldn't it be wonderful if those whose lives we touched remembered us with honor and respect long after our earthly existence has ended? What are you doing to insure that this will happen with your descendants?

> *We don't inherit the earth from our ancestors; we borrow it from our children.* David Brewer

Most of us have a conventional view of time. People who come earlier pass on ideas, values and the earth itself to those who come later. It is hard to conceive of anything different, isn't it? What if this idea is backwards? Think about this: what we possess now is really being borrowed from future generations. How we treat the world's resources and our fellow human beings now dramatically affects those who follow us. In other words, those of us living today are merely borrowing from the future as Mr. Brewer suggests. Do you think we might take better care of our environment, strive to establish peace throughout the world and create a place of love, joy and peace for those coming later? This type of thinking will help to eliminate the idea of, "I've got mine—I don't care what happens next." Thank you, future generations, for loaning us the wonders of the world we live in today.

You don't have to make it big, but you do have to make a big impact. Jamie McCall

There are exceptional people who make a giant mark during their lifetimes. Think of Saints Peter and Paul, Thomas Aquinas, Abraham Lincoln, Thomas Edison, Martin Luther King, Jr. and Pope John Paul II among many others. For most of the rest of us, our lives are lived below society's radar screen. We may be important and loved by family and friends but otherwise anonymous outside our small circle. The point is we don't have to be written up in prestigious history books or have our statues in public halls around the world to make a significant impact on the lives of those we touch. By our words and actions, we teach others about love, the presence of God in our life, how to lead upright and productive lives and all the other things that are truly important in life. Hopefully, we do this well in spite of our many human frailties. Even though only a few people will recognize your name in the obituary page of the local newspaper, the impact your life had on others was profound and positive. Every one of us can aspire to make a big impact on some people.

Love today the way you want to be remembered tomorrow Dillon Burroughs

We cannot expect to be unlovable in life and also remembered lovingly when we are departed. In the first chapter of this book, we spoke about the importance of love. Of all the virtues, it is the most precious. Do you extend love to every person in your life today?

# # #

What does this chapter mean to our spiritual journey? We must do our best to live life in an exemplary way, one that makes us a model for those we influence. We try to do that in spite of our human weaknesses. Even the most flawed among us still have the capacity to love others. In the final analysis, your own spiritual journey will be most affected by how you have loved others. We may often fail because of our pettiness, anger or judgmentalism. Yet, we must try. That's what our individual legacy will be all about—did you do your best to love God and your neighbor wherever or whoever he or she may be?

CHAPTER 9

HOW ABOUT PEACE AND ACCEPTANCE IN THE FACE OF LOSS?

Most of us admire those who exhibit consistent serenity and calm especially when immersed in events that are not tranquil. Our feelings of esteem also extend to folks that quietly and heroically accept what life deals to them even though the circumstances of the events may be personally painful or tragically jarring. It is much more common to observe people who seem constantly fretful about the trials of life they must endure. These folks may angrily explode with, "Why me?" when events turn sour and the black clouds of difficulty invade their lives.

Which of these two groups of people—those who exhibit peace and equanimity or those who lash out in anger at their fate—offer a model for our own spiritual existence? Our scriptural knowledge reminds us that Jesus frequently exhorted his disciples to be at peace. Many of the great biblical figures were also known for accepting the difficulties they faced with stoicism. Does that mean people who are full of peace and acceptance possess some super-human traits or virtues? Probably not. They may have been anxious, wounded by events swirling about them and full of fears and doubts—just like you and me. But, somehow they were able to put their circumstances into a God-centered context and gained their strength and acceptance by recognizing they were not in control. Turning things over to God may be the key to gaining peace and accepting loss gracefully. What do you think about this idea?

HAVE I EXPERIENCED PEACE IN MY LIFE?

A large proportion of mature adults speak about feeling a general sense of unease in their lives. Many things contribute to this. First of all, life in general seems to be frenetic with things happening too fast to process. There are worries about health in the present and how it may deteriorate in the future. Issues about family relationships, and the lives being lived by children and grandchildren create concerns. Money and the possibility of outliving financial resources can create a sense of dread; having to move in with adult children and rely upon them financially would represent a serious loss of personal control of one's life to some.

There may even be increasing anxiety about the afterlife that may now seem close. Have I really been forgiven for my past sins? Is there a possibility that I could face an eternity of damnation? Must I die alone? Will the step across the threshold from this life to the next be peaceful, taken as I am surrounded with loving family and friends—or wretchedly painful and lonely? In your own life, there may be other issues that make sought-after peace obscure for you. Certainly peace is something we all desire; and we don't want it to be elusive, to come and go. Peace: How can we achieve it and make it a part of our psychological makeup?

Peace begins with a smile. Mother Teresa

It seems to me that none of us can achieve any degree of peace with a grumpy disposition. So, we might consider taking advice from Mother Teresa. Let us start our quest for peace by keeping a determined smile on our faces in spite of circumstances that might be upsetting to us. If nothing else, the people we encounter may wonder why we look so happy in the midst of a less than pleasant situation. "What does that person know that I don't?" they may ask after seeing your smiling countenance.

You cannot find peace by avoiding life. Virginia Woolf

When our peace is threatened it may seem convenient to play ostrich, that is, to bury our heads and pretend that bad things are not happening around us. But that just doesn't work. We live in the world with other people, with circumstances, with situations beyond our control. If peace is to be found, it must happen with those things swirling around us. Attempts to wall off the reality of life are fruitless.

Peace comes from within. Do not seek it without. Gautama Buddha

You can look everywhere outside yourself seeking an experience of peace. You will not find it. As the old French proverb says, "life is an onion and one peels it crying." Some of us may be uncomfortable peeling off the layers that cover our inmost self. We don't want to look at some of the disreputable things that could be deeply buried there. But it is only at this core place that we will ever find true peace.

You find peace not by rearranging the circumstances of your life, but by realizing who you are at the deepest level of your being. Eckhart Tolle

When attempting to change ourselves in a fundamental way, we usually start with external things, believing that by changing these we can affect a fundamental change in our spirit. Peace is not to be found in exterior components. Peace is deeply buried in the heart of our being. If and when we experience peace in our lives, it will spring from the center of our souls. The peace you find will be determined by who you are in your spirit center.

Peace is not something you wish for, it is something you make, something you are, something you do, and something you give away. Robert Fulghum

People have said to me—and I have said to myself—"I wish I was more at peace." As Mr. Fulghum said wishing won't help. We need to find the means to make peace a fundamental part of our lives. A big portion of our success in finding peace will depend on how we act in daily life and our ability to harness our own strengths, weaknesses, faults and talents to create a true and lasting peace in our spirit. If we are fortunate to capture this prize of peace, we are also reminded that we may not jealously horde it. If you are blessed with peace, give it away to others in your life. You will find that it is like the loaves and fishes. Your generosity will not diminish your abundance.

The day I understood everything was the day I stopped trying to figure everything out. The day I finally knew peace was the day I let everything go.
C. JoyBell C.

Just when we think we finally have all the pieces put together and the situation in hand, we come to the sudden realization that God is—and has always been—in control. What a liberating conclusion this is! For most of our lives we feel we are firmly in charge, skillfully directing our own fate even when the road ahead is hazy and full of unexpected turns. That's the way we like it; we do not want to cede this personal control to anyone else. Then we determine—finally—that's not the way things work. Once we are able to let go and turn things over to God, peace flows into our soul as a silent midnight fog creeps into a summer garden.

Peace is present right here and now, in ourselves and in everything we do and see. Every breath we take, every step we take, can be filled with peace, joy, serenity. The question is whether or not we are in touch with it. We need only to be awake, alive in the present moment. Thich Nhat Hanh

Many of us find peace of mind to be indefinable and vague. It's like looking all over the house for your reading glasses without luck and then finding them an hour later perched on your head. Peace is so elusive to us and yet it is right in front of us, an integral part of us built into the fabric of our being. All of us may have to peel back some layers to find it, but it is there "alive in the present moment." God can show you where your peace can be found.

Peace is the gift of God. Do you want peace? Go to God. Do you want peace in your families? Go to God.
John Taylor

Were you hoping for a different answer about the nature of personal peace? No, it is the same thing as with most of our needs; we need God's help to achieve the peace we so earnestly seek. We not only need God, He is eager to help us. So, as Mr. Taylor says, go to God and ask Him for that which we seek.

Do not be afraid to take a chance on peace, to teach peace, to live peace. Peace is the last word of history. Pope John Paul II

If you find peace, great; but you are not allowed to keep it to yourself. The second part of this human equation? Share it with others. Can you conceive of anything better than peace spreading from person to person until the whole world experiences this gift of God? If that ever did happen, it would certainly be writ large as "the last word of history," as the Great John Paul II said.

Courage is the price life extracts for granting peace.
Amelia Earhart

In virtually every human endeavor, courage is a fundamental component. Peace never happens by itself. For any person to achieve peace, courage must be exhibited. Gaining peace often requires us to stretch our boundaries, to venture into unknown places. While we pray for peace, we must also ask God for courage to recognize it and grasp it when we find it.

The two most important things in life are real love and being at peace with yourself. Jonathon Carroll

The following five "timeless thoughts," practical suggestions for achieving inner peace, were found on the Internet:[9]

- <u>Simplify</u>. For example, keep your to-do lists to 2-3 items only; set strict time limits for yourself to check daily email or interact with Facebook, Twitter and other social media sites.

- <u>Accept</u>. Accept what is and stop using energy resisting what is. This doesn't mean giving up. It merely means focusing your energy on what is needed to change your situation for the better.

- <u>Forgive</u>. Forgiveness helps one to let go of things. When you don't forgive, you are still linked to the offending person. And, don't forget to forgive yourself too, which is as important as forgiving another.

- <u>Do What You Enjoy</u>. Peace naturally flows to people who like what they do whether that be work, avocation, hobby or leisure activities. Not sure what really pleases you? Explore life, try things out, see what makes you happy.

- <u>Be Careful With Peace</u>. Don't be in a hurry, do things quietly and calmly. Be smart and practice living in the present moment.

ACCEPTANCE IN THE FACE OF LOSS

Acceptance and *loss* are two distinct concepts. Yet, they seem to be inexorably linked. In this section of the book, we will alternate writing about these two ideas. It is up to you, dear reader, to tie them together based on your own experiences and circumstances. May this task be fruitful for your spiritual life.

Grief does not change you. It reveals you.
John Green

No human being goes through life without experiencing grief. Many will say that the loss of a mother, father, child or dearest friend changes them forever. But, as Mr. Green says, perhaps what we think is change may really be the opening of a window into our hearts to show our true character. Do you see grief as a normal occurrence in life? How have you dealt with it in the past? When tragedy strikes, do you view it as an undeserved punishment from God?

Understanding is the first key to acceptance, and only with acceptance can there be eventual recovery. J. K. Rowling

"I just don't understand why this tragedy has befallen me. What did I do to deserve such a misfortune?" We have all heard this before, and possibly have said it ourselves. It is a question derived from a disordered view of the human condition. No one has special credentials to exempt him or her from the blows life sometimes delivers to every human being. We are called to understand. Each of us necessarily takes a turn receiving heartbreak or calamity of some sort. Once we admit the truth of this proposition, our acceptance will lead to eventual recovery as Ms. Rowling says.

Mostly it is loss that teaches us about the worth of things. Arthur Schopenhauer

Have you ever cut the thumb on your dominant hand? It is only such an accident that dramatically demonstrates how important your injured thumb is to the performance of so many daily chores. That analogy works for most losses we face. Only after we have suffered loss do we recognize how important this deficit is. It is an unfortunate truth that most of us take a lot for granted—people, places and things. What would be your greatest loss if taken away from you?

Life is a series of natural and spontaneous changes. Don't resist them; that only causes sorrow. Let reality be reality. Lao Tzu

Everyone who reaches maturity has learned that life is a series of ups and downs. The cycles can be charted like sine waves on an oscilloscope. The trick in your life is not to let the peaks get too high or the valleys too low. They are going to happen no matter what. As the philosopher says, don't fight it; let reality happen.

The amazing thing about loss is instead of making you weak, it gives you strength. Rhianna Ryder

We often think that a devastating loss is like a body blow that weakens the recipient. Most often, that is not the case. A new patina of toughness envelopes us when we accept loss and recognize that life continues. This is not a flinty hardness but something that makes us more gentle and pliable in God's loving hands. This requires acceptance of God's plan for our life. Have you reached that acceptance yet?

Wisdom is knowing what you have to accept.
Wallace Stegner

I think most of us would like to be considered wise, full of wisdom. Must we accept everything that comes our way as implied above? No, that is an incorrect interpretation of the material. When we are beset with social or economic injustice, persecution for who we are or what we stand for or ridiculed and treated with contempt because of our strongly held beliefs, we have no obligation to accept these things. On the contrary, we should vigorously resist these types of injustices. As Mr. Stegner suggests, wisdom is knowing what we have to accept as a part of the rhythm of living life. When this balance is achieved, may you be called a wise person.

The most beautiful people I've known are those who have known trials, struggles and loss, and have found their way out of the depths.
Elizabeth Kubler-Ross

Ms. Kubler-Ross has written movingly about the six stages of grief that many people experience. This brief quote distills her observations very well. When we battle through the pain of grief and loss—and often it is a real battle—we may find a gentle soul, beautiful in nature who is calm, caring and very considerate of others. Some of the most difficult events of our lives may provide us wonderful opportunities to become special human beings, full of love and compassion for others. Have you experienced this after some devastating loss that invaded your life?

Many of us crucify ourselves between two thieves—regret for the past and fear of the future.
Fulton Oursler

I find great symbolism in this quote. Many of us cannot let go of the past. We continue to dwell on prior pain and loss trying to wring more regret from unpleasant experiences. Then we constantly dither about what the future holds, feeling sure that almost all scenarios possible will be negative. All of us need to stop crucifying ourselves this way. Only the present moment counts for anything. Are you guilty of useless focus on what has gone before and what has yet to come? Stop it!

I know now that we never get over great losses. We absorb them and they carve us into different, often kinder, creatures. Gail Caldwell

Much has been written about getting past our losses. The fact remains that we never really get over some events. If we turn things over to God, we may be able to endure these difficult events in a way that softens us. Have you been successful?

It is best to accept life as it really is and not as I imagined it to be. Paulo Coelho

Most young people have an idealized view of what their lives will be like. As they mature, they often discover that life isn't always fair or easy; what they expected life to be may not measure up to their ideal. That may be a valuable lesson in maturity. How we imagine things may not be realistic; that's okay. It helps to be more pragmatic about how life really is. You don't have to give up your dreams; don't demand the perfect and be willing to live with the good.

To be a follower of the Crucified means sooner or later, a personal encounter with the cross. And the cross always entails loss. Elisabeth Elliot

For the believing Christian, Good Friday is always followed by Easter and resurrection. Before that glorious Sunday feast occurs, we must have our own personal meeting at the foot of the cross. Like Jesus, many of us must absorb real pain and loss. No matter how difficult that may be for us, we are assured of a resurrection experience. It has been said that the lives of many are filled with Good Friday and Easter situations. Think of the many times you have felt devastated by life's events. While enormously painful, you came out the other side stronger and ready to begin anew. Jesus said, "Come to me all you who are burdened and I will give you rest." Do you believe that The Lord was including you in that promise?

Sometimes in life there is no problem and sometime there is no solution. Within this space—between these poles—life exists. Rasheed Ogunlaru

Yes, life has ebbs and flows. It is amazing that we experience long stretches when things are good, problems seem to be in the background and we don't have to deal with difficulties. Naturally, all of us appreciate those times. We know from sacred scripture, "This, too, shall pass." Many of us have had a sudden transition from "no problem" to "no solution." The quote rightly states that our lives exist between these two extremes. The key point to remember is that nothing stays the same forever. Enjoy the good times; deal with the difficulties. That's what life is.

Everything that has a beginning has an ending.
Make your peace with that and all will be well.
Gautama Buddha

This is a perfect quote to end this section. The cycle of life and death is immutable and endless. Once we really own this concept, life becomes easier.

# # #

Peace, loss and acceptance: They are principal ingredients in the recipe for living one's life. The road we traverse on our salvation journey will present inevitable situations where loss occurs requiring our eventual acceptance of the reality life has dealt us. We are blessed if peace wraps us in its gentle arms along the way. When you consider your own personal journey, try to figure out how you will experience "peace that surpasses all understanding" and gentle acceptance in the face of those rocky patches we all face in life. With God's abiding grace and presence within you, we each can find meaning and purpose for the lives we lead.

Greg Hadley

CHAPTER 10

HOW AM I CARING FOR THE TEMPLE OF THE HOLY SPIRIT?

In a previous chapter on the topic of *Spiritual Life and Personal Prayer,* it was stipulated that every human being is composed of a finite body and an immortal soul. We cannot separate our body and soul—they are seamlessly connected, and both represent a glorious gift to us from Almighty God. We must conclude, therefore, that our human bodies have a profound spiritual component. As we read in St. Paul's first letter to the Corinthians, "Your body is the Temple of the Holy Spirit...glorify God in your body." And, so we must.

The spiritual nature of our soul is easy to understand. The spiritual nature of our body may be more difficult to grasp. We know that every living creature experiences bodily death. Our intellect readily acknowledges, "You are dust and to dust you will return," even though we might not relish the end result. What can possibly be so spiritual about our bodies? At best we live four score and ten—a little less, a little more—and then return to the earth. The key to our comprehension comes when we accept that The Triune God actually dwells within us. Think carefully about this. God does not reside in some infinitely distant place we call heaven. No, God is everywhere and that includes inside each and every one of us. To appreciate this may be extraordinarily difficult for some people. "How could God possibly take up residence inside me? I am so unworthy and unlovable; I just can't believe this can be true!" This may be the reaction of many—including yourself, perhaps? Thanks be to God, it is true! Our human bodies are holy temples where God—Father, Son and Spirit—resides. When this truth is accepted, each of us must assume a different view of our own human bodies.

What kind of view are we talking about? If it's true that we are Temples of God, how does that change the way we care for our bodies? Most of us would probably have a mental picture of a temple as a gleaming place, beautifully constructed with every surface polished, pristine and sparkling clean. That model temple, just described, has no relationship to how we view our own bodies. A cursory glance into a full-length mirror may reveal a body that is overweight, losing hair, with diminished sight, flat feet, arthritic hands and the entire package covered with mottled skin. That description may be 'way too harsh for many but some of us don't resemble temples very much, do we? Doesn't God love each of us unconditionally whether we are tall or short, fat or skinny, young or old, beautiful or less so? Yes, God does love each of us but that does not diminish our requirement to care for our bodies.

Where does this requirement on us emanate? The tablet Moses brought down from the mountain included the commandment, "Thou Shalt Not Kill." This implies not only fatal harm to others but doing harm to ourselves. Yes, this commandment calls upon each of us to take appropriate care of our own bodies by consuming sensible amounts of nutritious food and drink, exercising on a regular basis suitable for our age and general condition, being reasonable about safety matters, not smoking, wearing our seat belts and proactively obtaining medical and dental care as needed. As mature, senior adults all the judicious diet restrictions and reasonable amounts of exercise may not produce a svelte, toned body. But, we are called to be the best Temple we can possibly be. This section of the book is not a scold about losing weight, exercising more or changing some life-long habits. It is about raising awareness that we are Temples and, as such, we should make these Temples as welcoming to God's indwelling as possible.

The first wealth is health. Ralph Waldo Emerson

The greatest source of human happiness is good health. If you don't believe this, speak with someone who suffers with a chronic illness, has recently had a devastating stroke or is dealing with a terminal disease. Good health is a major component of a good life, one that is led productively, happily and with a purpose. Most often, good health is not an accident; one has to work to obtain and maintain this blessing.

When health is absent, wisdom cannot reveal itself, art cannot manifest, strength cannot fight, wealth becomes useless and intelligence cannot be applied.
Herophilus

You may have experienced this yourself. Overtaken by poor health, you may feel depressed, confused and unfocused. Your productivity drops, you often feel listless and weak. You may not be thinking straight and tasks formerly easy for you to accomplish now represent difficult, time-consuming chores. Many undesirable side effects flow from poor health. No one wants to experience this. Shouldn't health be a priority for your life?

Get comfortable with being uncomfortable.
Jillian Michaels

It is easy to get used to the many creature comforts available in our generally affluent society. Many of us don't walk much anymore; the auto is too convenient. Compared to former generations, we eat a lot of meals away from home. None of these things contribute to robust health. All of us need to understand that restricting the intake of calories and expending energy on physical activity can be a little uncomfortable. The fitness expert, Ms. Michaels, provides wise counsel: get comfortable with being uncomfortable. Doing so will lead us to healthier and happier lives.

It is easier to change a man's religion than to change his diet. Margaret Mead

If you conclude that changes must be made in your own life, it is important to be realistic about the obstacles you will face in reaching your goals. Deciding to lose a few pounds in order to improve health is a worthy objective. It's also hard to do. Most of us have become pretty habitual about our eating habits. Go slow, set realistic targets and don't give up the first time you "fall off the wagon." Creating a nice temple for God is a very good thing to strive for. Ask God for the strength, courage and persistence you need.

Thinking about working out burns zero calories, zero percentage of fat and accomplishes zero goals.
Gwen Ro

We read. We contemplate meaning. We begin to understand what we must do. Now is the time to actually perform. Reflection and consideration must be put behind us. As Ms. Ro points out, nothing actually happens until we do something concrete. Are you ready? Let's get started today; there is absolutely no reason to wait. Our temples need polishing!

> **Sorry—there is no magic bullet. You gotta eat healthy and live healthy to be healthy and look healthy. End of story**. Morgan Spurlock

Hope is eternal. We carefully—almost frantically—scan the weekly magazines or television advertising for the latest and greatest diet pill guaranteed to help us lose weight. We also search for the vibrating belt that tones our muscles or the "sauna shirt" that lets us shed unwanted pounds. Mr. Spurlock dashes these unrealistic hopes and tells us like it really is: you have to do it yourself because there are no magic bullets to be found. You already knew this but it does make it a little easier to get to work on our own temples.

> **When it comes to eating right and exercising, there is no, "I'll start tomorrow." Tomorrow is a disease.**
> Terri Guillemets

It may be true that the greatest obstacle to changing our lives is tomorrow. We rationalize that we'll do all those things we need to do, but we can't start today so we'll get going tomorrow. Why is it that we can never find time today but there will always be time tomorrow? Again, we know this is nothing more than an excuse but we use it anyway. When Paul told the Corinthians to "Glorify God in your bodies" he meant starting today.

It is in the balancing of your spirituality with your humanity that you will find immeasurable happiness, success and good health. Steve Maraboli

In most human endeavors, balance is an important element. When we achieve the proper mix between our spiritual life and our humanity, this normally leads us to happiness, success and health. The point is this: We must avoid over-emphasis on either aspect of our dual natures. Leading the life of a remote spiritual hermit or eagerly clinging to human activities probably is not the proper course for most people. What things do you do in your own life to maintain a spiritual and human values balance?

The only pushup you won't be able to do is the one you never do. Gwen Ro

I once heard a comedian say, "I'm not in good enough condition to get into shape." Sometimes I hear my friends say the same thing. As we age, the creaky condition of our knees, shortness of breath or just a general lack of stamina discourages us from even beginning a fitness improvement program. Setting unrealistic goals is the real problem in most cases. We visualize we can go from bad to good physical condition in a short time. In reality, we must take "baby steps" on any fitness agenda. Slow and easy must be the watchword. Don't let yourself be deterred. Take your time. Results will follow. It can take a long time to build a beautiful temple.

Love yourself enough to take care of your health of mind, body and soul as a top priority, then you will be fit to face anything. Jay Woodman

Once again, we return to the necessity for self love. Too many of us don't think we are very lovable either to ourselves or to others. God has repeatedly indicated His love for us is infinite and unconditional. By failing to love ourselves, we imply that God has made a defective human being. We know that is not the case. Our love of self must include a commitment to care for our body and mind as well as our soul. When every element of our being is in good condition, Mr. Woodman suggests we will be ready for any challenge.

The traditional approach to an unknown risk is avoidance. James F. Clapp

and

Whenever I feel the need to exercise, I lie down until it goes away. Paul Terry

These last two wisdom quotes are a lighthearted look at our topic. The first quote from Mr. Clapp brings to mind another bromide: "Hard work and exercise never killed anyone, but why take the chance?" The second quote speaks for itself. We end on this amusing note because we don't want this chapter to come across as a stern lecture about what someone else thinks you should do. The main point is our affirmation that our bodies truly are Temples of the Holy Spirit. As such, we have an obligation to take care of ourselves appropriately and avoid life style choices that may be abusive.

Greg Hadley

CHAPTER 11

HOW HAVE I PREPARED FOR DEATH AND THE AFTERLIFE?

The greatest event of life is death. Intellectually, all of us know that we must face the end of our earthly life eventually. While we are alive and robust, the end of life seems to be on a gauzy, far distant horizon. Some, because of serious health issues or advanced age, may discover a sharper focus as the end comes closer. Still others will be oblivious until a sudden catastrophic accident or health event snuffs out a life. So, death comes to each of us. In the normal course of events death arrives in our old age but we sadly know too well the stories of children, young people and others taken before their time. The question is: What does death mean and how are we prepared for this terminal event?

We often refer to death as "the end." To those who believe each human being is comprised of a finite body and an immortal soul, death takes on a different meaning. When a person expires, his or her loved ones, family and friends are saddened by the loss of human contact. There will be no more conversations, hugs, good times, companionship and interaction with the one who has passed away. However, there is hope and faith that the person's immortal soul lives on in a different state. We consign those who have lived a devout and pious life, full of love for others, utilizing their gifts in service to fellow humans to a place in God's keeping where they will be happy for all eternity. That blissful hope is given to each of us, even though we are flawed humans who make our share of mistakes. The problem that worries us is that we may not have measured up during our lives to God's call that we love Him and our neighbors as He has loved us. What happens to those of us who have failed miserably to live the command to love God and neighbor? We do not know with certainty since no one has returned from the grave to inform us except Jesus, the resurrected God/Man. During our lives, many of us discover and admit our transgressions and repent, reconciling with our God Whom we have offended or our neighbor. Even then, there is always the niggling doubt that we may have turned our back on God or failed in our neighborly duties along the way. How will God treat us when we meet Him face to face after our death? While hopeful, we are unsure. We also know God has given each of us a free will. He does not force us to live our lives in accordance with His will. Is it possible for us to separate ourselves from God forevermore? Yes, it probably is. Our greatest hope is that God, who is all-merciful, will treat us gently when we pass through the veil.

Many will say they do not fear death. While that may be true, when we consider the circumstances surrounding our death we may become quite anxious. While all would like to pass away quietly during sleep, most dread the possibilities of a fiery auto accident, drowning, a fall from a high place or an agonizingly painful disease. Unfortunately, the primary cause of death is not ours to decide so we must condition ourselves to accept the ending God sends. As Dr. Sherwin Nuland wrote, "The greatest dignity to be found in death is the dignity of the life that preceded it."[10]

While we may worry about the actual situation of our death our focus should be on the life we live. Have we done our best? Have we cooperated with God's graces? Did we utilize our gifts to build the Kingdom of God on earth? This is what truly matters. Our abiding hope is that when we pass from this life to the next, God will not check us for medals awarded for our perfection but for scars from all our attempts to lead a holy, productive and loving life to the best of our ability. Please, dear God, be merciful to us when we meet You at life's end. You called us to sainthood; let us live forever in Your presence. May the redemptive power of Your passion and death, O Lord, open the gates of heaven for each of us.

Dying? It's not the end of everything. We think it is. But what happens on earth is only the beginning.
Mitch Albom

It is painful to attend some funerals or memorial services. The survivors of the deceased are so distraught that only their tortured grief is on display. This sometimes occurs when the family has no special religious belief. To them, death is a final desolation, a bitter ending where hope does not exist. While a sense of loss and grief are normal at these times there should also exist celebration, tearful joy and thanks for a life (hopefully) well lived. To believers, death is not the end but the beginning, as Mr. Albom points out. Let each of us ask for the grace to deal with death in a hopeful and expectant way.

Death is contagious.
It is contracted the moment we are conceived.
Madeleine L'Engle

It is well for us to remember this idea throughout our lives. When we are young we feel "bullet proof" and the idea of death rarely receives our attention. Even in middle age, or older, many deny death except those who suffer with serious illness or disabilities. And, yet, we all die sooner or later. Since believers know that judgment follows death, it would be prudent for each of us to remember daily the fragility of life. While not suggesting that anyone should have a morbid sense of death being around every corner, we should recall that God gave us the gift of life for a purpose. The Catechism says we are here "To know, love and serve God in this life and be happy with Him forever in the next." Is this a focus of your daily prayer and a template for how you are living your life each day?

The fear of death follows from a fear of life. The person who lives fully is prepared to die at any time. Mark Twain

How do we best prepare for death and the afterlife? Leading a full, rich, robust, loving and productive life is the best answer. God has given each of us the gift of life. Along with that He has provided us with unique talents and charisms. Instead of hanging back, we must use freely what God has given freely to us. Those of us who try to do this every single day are probably best prepared to face the end of life whenever it arrives. Do you feel you have used your life and talents to the best of your ability? Then all is well.

One lives in hope of becoming a memory.
Antonio Porchiaand

and

To live in the hearts we leave behind is not to die.
Thomas Campbell

How do you hope to be remembered by your loved ones, family and friends after your death? Each of us would hope to be remembered for our loving attitude, a sense of justice and fairness toward all, a commitment to honesty, a sense of humor and personal integrity. If that is what we want as our legacy, we must lead our lives accordingly...it's that simple. As the quotes say, each of us wishes to be remembered. And, when we are, we have not died.

It is death that provides life with all its meaning.[11]
M. Scott Peck M.D.

History is written after the fact. The true meaning of an individual life often becomes clear only after the person has died. The profound climax of death is full of many different meanings. Our lives are like a stage production. When the final curtain is lowered, how will others view your performance? Will those in our sphere during life remember us as having used our gifts to build the Kingdom? Will we be fondly remembered as living a life of compassion for others, justice for all and love of neighbors? The wise know that heaven cannot be earned; only the redemptive power of the Cross can open heaven's gate for us. We also know that our works, supported by God's grace, represents our response to God's redemptive power. Will our effort be worthy of the world's applause? And God's?

# # #

What do we take away from this chapter to assist us on our salvation journey? Human death represents the punch line and closes the period when we can accept or reject the divine grace manifested in Jesus Christ. Christians believe that each person receives a particular judgment at the very moment of death—deliverance into the blessedness of heaven, through purification or immediately, or everlasting damnation. Heaven is referred to as the ultimate end and fulfillment of the deepest human longings, the state of supreme, definitive happiness. To achieve this euphoric state requires that we spend our earthly lives cooperating with divine grace, doing our utmost to love God and our neighbor and leading a moral, upright and righteous life.

Each of us knows that directing our life in this manner can represent a real challenge. Each one of us is weak, flawed, mistake prone and frequently unloving. Even the great saints were human and experienced periods of discouragement and spiritual failure in their lives. To become the person God wants us to be requires a complete reliance on His grace and mercy, a humility that we can do nothing without Him and utter thankfulness for the gifts he has bestowed on us. To sum up, we must strive to follow the roadmap God has given to each of us. Our human lives are relatively short and despite many distractions we must do our best to keep focused on our true objective: To live a human life that permits our immortal soul to spend all eternity in the glorious presence of Almighty God.

To sum up, Gilda Radner, television actress and comedienne wrote, "I wanted a perfect ending. Now I've learned, the hard way, that some poems don't rhyme, some stories don't have a clear beginning, middle and end. Life is about not knowing, having to change, taking a moment and making the best of it without knowing what is going to happen next. Delicious ambiguity..."

I hope this little book has helped you program your spiritual G.P.S. so that your personal salvation journey may be direct and not face too many detours. May God abundantly bless you, filling your spirit with love.

Greg Hadley

REFERENCES

- Unless otherwise noted, all Wisdom Quotes can be found at the following Internet website: www.goodreads.com/quotes/

- All Biblical scripture passages are taken from The New American Bible, Thomas Nelson Publishers, Nashville, TN

CHAPTER	REFERENCE NUMBER	REFERENCE
Preface	1	M. Scott Peck, MD. "The Road Less Traveled," Touchstone Books, New York City, NY
1	2	Dale Alquist. "The Apostle of Common Sense." Ignatius Press, San Francisco, CA
2	3	Father Richard Berg, CSC. "Fragments of Hope." Corby Books, Notre Dame, IN
3	4	www.gotquestions.org Got Questions Ministry.
3	5	Fr. Richard Berg, CSC and Christine McCarthy. "Depression and the Integrated Life" Alba House Publishing, New York City, NY
3	6	Ibid
3	7	Gregory Boyle, S.J. "Tattoos on the Heart." Free Press Books, New York City, NY

CHAPTER	REFERENCE NUMBER	REFERENCE
4	8	William Paul Young. "The Shack." Windblown Media, Newberry Park, CA
9	9	www.positivityblog.com
11	10	Sherwin Nuland. "How We Die." Vintage Books, New York City, NY
11	11	M. Scott Peck, MD, "The Road Less Traveled" Touchstone Books, New York City, NY

ABOUT THE AUTHOR

Greg Hadley with his wife, Evelyn, lives in Lake Oswego, Oregon in a retirement community. The couple has six children and fourteen grandchildren.

After completing his undergraduate education at the University of San Francisco, finishing his MBA studies at Pepperdine University, and attending the Harvard Business School, Greg spent his professional life in the business world. He worked for IBM and was General Manager of Computer Sciences of Australia. Then, for twenty years, Hadley and his partners acquired, operated and sold industrial companies. Moving from California to Oregon in 1990 Greg established a management consulting practice, spent time as a college educator, author, and professional public speaker. Greg continues to spend time in civic, political and community volunteer activities.

Hadley spent thirty-nine years as an amateur baseball umpire, mostly at the NCAA Division 1 level. He has authored seven books prior to this one.

Please see the list of titles at the beginning of this book. For further information, visit the website www.gbhadley.com.

Made in the USA
San Bernardino, CA
31 October 2013